BEFORE REALITY HITS

A Straightforward Guide to College Success

MEGAN ANN SMITH

This book is presented for educational purposes only. This book is intended to be applicable to information relating to most United States colleges and may not be applicable to colleges outside the United States. This book is comprised of the opinions and ideas of the author. The information, methods, and recommendations outlined in this book may not be appropriate for every person, and are not guaranteed or warranted to produce any outcomes or results. By publishing this book, the author and the publisher are not engaged in the execution or provision of any professional service, to include legal, accounting, or any other professional service.

Every precaution was taken in the preparation of this book. However, the author and publisher assume no responsibility for errors or omissions, or for damages that may result from the use of information contained herein. No guarantee or warranty is made regarding the accuracy or completeness of the information contained in this book. The author and the publisher assume no responsibility for any liability, loss, or risk, which may be incurred as a result of the use or application of any of the contents herein.

Published by Sally Sue Enterprises LLC
http://www.sallysueenterprisesllc.com

ISBN-10: 0615805329
ISBN-13: 9780615805320

DEDICATION

To my mother, father, and grandfather for teaching me that through hard work and determination all things are possible. You will always be my heroes.

CONTENTS

ACKNOWLEDGMENTS

There are several people whom I must recognize for their support. First and foremost I must thank my family. To my mother, father, grandfather, sisters, and brother-in-law, thank you for always supporting me. Without you, there is no doubt in my mind that I would not be where I am today. Thank you for providing me continual opportunities and always challenging me to succeed.

Closely behind my family are my closest friends who have always believed in me. To Elise, thank you for always believing in me and making me a better person. And to Kevin, thank you for your support, patience, and fortitude over the last several years.

In addition to my family and friends, I have had several mentors over the years who have helped me considerably, not only when it came to getting my foot in the door, landing interviews, internships, and full-time positions, but who have guided my overall career progression. To Mike, Mike, Randy, and Ray, thank you. Your help has not gone unnoticed and I hope to someday be able to mentor some-one else to the same level you have mentored me. Thank you for guiding me and providing me with the tools for success.

INTRODUCTION

I am no one special. I wasn't born into an affluent family. I am not a celebrity. And yet I was able to attend college, graduate a semester early, have my student loans paid off in less than two and a half years, complete my master's degree for free, and achieve my goal of a six-figure salary by age twenty-three. So what is my secret? Planning ahead, hard work, and determination. It really is that simple.

Whether you are the parent of a child approaching high school graduation, the parent of a child currently in college, someone considering going back to school, or a student yourself, this book can assist you in making the most of college to ensure you choose an appropriate college based on your career goals and financial situation, help you prepare for internships throughout college, and graduate with the foundation required to land in your desired career field without an unmanageable amount of student loan debt. For the purposes of this book, the terms school and college are used interchangeably.

The vast majority of the students I attended college with graduated without a job lined up, and many of them are still jobless or working oddball jobs trying to make ends meet. To make matters worse, nearly all of them have student loan debt that they are struggling severely to keep up with. My goal with this book is to ensure that you are not this student upon graduation. This book is a no-nonsense approach to college, with simple steps you can take to avoid the common pitfalls experienced by a significant number of college students.

WHERE TO APPLY

For those of you still in high school or those that are deciding now is the time to go back to school, the task of selecting an appropriate college is quite daunting. There are literally hundreds of colleges to choose from and several questions you must answer: Public or private? In-state or out-of-state? How many schools should I apply to? What about online education?

As you begin to answer these questions, the most important rule is to limit the number of colleges you apply to. I recommend limiting yourself to ten applications, inclusive of two backup schools. Anything beyond ten is frivolous; it indicates that you really have no idea where you want to go or what you want to do. Beyond that, applications cost money and add up quickly. According to a September 2012 *US News & World Report* article, "the average cost of application fees that the 1,391 ranked colleges provided in spring 2012—the most recent year that *US News* collected data— was $37.88, when not adjusted for schools' reduced online application fees."[1] Therefore, if you stick to only ten applications you should expect to spend approximately $378.80 in application costs. Keep in mind that this is an approximate number based on averages, so you might spend more or less depending on your school selection list. This same *US News & World Report* article also points out that schools may have "online application fees" that can be "considerably lower," so always check to see if an online application is an available option that can save you money during the application process.[2]

Limiting yourself to ten applications is not only an important exercise in forcing you to make realistic decisions about where you want to go and what you want to be when you grow up, but it is the first of many steps you should take to budget your money and save.

Ten applications is more than enough to apply to your backup schools, most likely candidates, as well as one or two long-shot dream schools that you have always wanted to apply to. If your list is over ten schools, keep reading, as the remainder of this chapter will assist you in narrowing down your list.

Understanding that you will only apply to ten colleges at most, the next question you must ask yourself is, how far from home are you willing to relocate? I myself couldn't wait to get away from home and gain independence. I ended up going to college a few states away, and while it did force me to grow up quickly and become independent, it made holidays much more difficult and expensive. In hindsight, I should have thought more about the consequences of moving farther away from home. So, if you are like me and excited to get away from home, be sure to consider how many times per year you plan to travel home. I would budget at least twice (for holidays), and remember that flight tickets are constantly going up in price. I would recommend you conduct a few searches online to determine what it would cost you per round trip ticket. You will need to look up these prices based on location for each school you plan to apply to and write them down (these prices will come in handy later as we determine the overall price of attending each college). If the college is within driving distance, calculate approximate miles and estimate the price it would cost you to drive home instead of fly.

In addition to thinking about how far away you would be during your college years, you also need to consider the possibility that where you decide to go to college could very well be the same location you obtain internships and job offers. So while you may be willing to move away for college, are you also willing to consider that location your long-term home? It is not uncommon that several of your internships and job opportunities will come from the same location as your college, so this is an important factor to consider. While it is possible to transfer locations after college, this can be complicated depending on current economic conditions and your career field. For example, if your career field is centralized in Texas and the majority of positions are only in Texas, relocating outside Texas after graduation may prove very difficult. On the other hand, if you plan to become an accountant, that is an occupation needed in most industries, thereby making location transfers in the future much easier. If you are looking at a specialized career field, ensure that the location(s) appeal to you. My career field is largely centered in the Washington,

DC, area, making a location transfer extremely difficult. As I am currently looking to move closer to my family in the Midwest, I sincerely wish I had thought more carefully about the specificity of my career field and inherent lack of job locations throughout the United States.

To help you make the decision about locations that you are willing to relocate to, you should generate a list of must haves and deal breakers when thinking about locations. For example, some people require humid locations for health reasons. This would then immediately rule out a location such as southern Arizona, which is notoriously dry year round. If you want to be within driving distance to home, then you will need to pull up a map and determine which states you consider being within driving distance and write those down. If, like me, you loathe commutes averaging one hour each way on a good day, locations such as Washington, DC, New York City, and Houston may not be the best option for you. Your goal should be to land in your desired career field while at the same time being in a geographic location where you will be content.

Now that you have an idea of where you want to be geographically, the next question you need to evaluate is, what do you want to study? Arguably, this is the most difficult question of all. With this question you will begin to head in the direction of your desired career, while simultaneously ruling out other possibilities. I found this to be one of the most difficult decisions because I knew that by selecting one area of study, I was intentionally shutting the door on other career possibilities. However, this is a part of growing up. You must begin to head down one path, not several. And while frightening, it is a very necessary step to making the most of college. If you already have an idea of what you want to do for a career, choosing an area of study and corresponding major will be quite simple.

If you don't yet know what you want to study, I recommend you make a list with two columns: Column A will contain items that you are good at, and Column B will contain items that you like to do. In theory, you want to highlight items that you are both good at and that you like to do. You want to choose an area of study that both interests you and that you will excel in. This is not an easy exercise. I recently completed this as part of a mentor program at my current job and found it quite difficult to find items that appeared in both columns that I could translate into additional careers or professional opportunities. Don't hold back on this list; include anything and everything that comes to mind. Some examples for me from Column A included playing piano, water skiing and sports in general, planning ahead, organizing, and studying languages. Column B included organizing, solving analytic problems, reading, cooking, and traveling. From your list you should start to see possible career paths. For example, if you included math in either column, perhaps accounting, finance, or statistics are career fields of interest to you, which would lead you to majors such as business, math, or economics (other majors could be applicable here as well). If you entered traveling and current events into either column, perhaps international studies or political science would be areas of study that are of interest to you, leading toward career paths such as politician, language translator, or analyst. If, after making this list, you are still at a loss for ideas, I recommend asking your parents, relatives, friends, and even some of your current teachers or mentors for input on your list. In my case, my friends and colleagues came up with other items that I failed to include on my list. These individuals might also have some ideas for careers they think you would be great at and simply haven't thought of yourself. I have included an example list below.

Table 1. Two-Column List

A WHAT I AM GOOD AT	B WHAT I LIKE TO DO
Playing Piano	Solving Analytic Problems
Water Skiing/Sports	Reading
Planning Ahead	Cooking/Baking
Organizing	Traveling
Studying Other Languages	Organizing
Managing Projects	Exercising

If you are someone thinking about going back to school and are currently in a job or career field, you need to decide whether you want to pursue your degree in an area of study to complement your current job, or whether you are hoping to change to a separate career field. If you are looking to complement your current job, conversations with your colleagues and supervisors should provide you with insight for a possible area of study. If you are looking to transfer career fields, you will need to conduct online research as outlined below.

If you are still having difficulty identifying an area of study, I recommend that you start looking at a few college websites and the different majors they offer. Start compiling a list of possible majors that seem intriguing and immediately delete anything that you know is not of interest to you. Keep this list with you and continue to cross off majors that are no longer of interest to you over time as you conduct additional research. Any majors that remain on the list should be explored further online to determine what type of careers they lead to. For example, if political science is still on the list as a possibility, I would conduct basic online searches on "political science careers" and see what types of jobs could result from political science. Repeat this process for all the majors on your list until you are able to narrow this list down to two or three possible majors.

And keep in mind that your major will not necessarily define you long term. Often people end up working in fields that have nothing to do with their undergraduate major. The important thing is to select a major that is of interest to you and will yield career opportunities that are of interest to you in the short term (the next five to ten years). When first entering the job market, it is likely that you will acquire a job relating to your major. After you are in the job market for a few years and have some experience to fall back on you should have an easier time switching to a job or career that is not closely related to your undergraduate major(s). Also remember that several majors, such as political science, are broad enough that they still leave a wide variety of career possibilities open.

Do not worry if this process takes awhile to complete. This is an important step and you want to make sure you identify an area of study and corresponding major that genuinely interest you. Do as much research as possible to make sure that the area of study you select aligns with your interests and goals. You may even want to consider speaking to any friends or relatives that majored in the same area. If you do not know of anyone that majored in one of the areas you are considering, call one of your local colleges (that you are actually considering applying to) and request to speak to a current student or recent graduate about this major. If you say you are considering this major and possibly attending their college, they are likely to put you in contact with a student either in person, over the phone, or online. Feel free to repeat this process at several colleges you are considering applying to if you want more information and different perspectives.

Once you have two or three majors and geographic locations of interest, you are now ready to begin selecting your ten schools to apply to. There are a few ways to do this. You can simply search for all the colleges within each state you are interested in moving to by using an online search engine. You can search by major using any online search engine as well. There are also several websites dedicated to producing lists of colleges that match your input criteria such as collegeview.com.[3] Another useful tool is usnews. com, which ranks colleges on various aspects.[4] I would recommend using at least two or three websites to ensure that they are providing you consistent results. If you get different results from the different websites, compile a list of all results in a spreadsheet and work from there. For example, if one website suggests that College XYZ would be perfect for you and another website lists College XYZ as a terrible fit for you, additional research is needed to determine whether you want to keep this college on your application list.

Once you have an initial list of schools, additional research is needed to finalize your list of ten schools. This research needs to be thorough so expect to spend a significant amount of time on this part of the process. For each school on the list, visit that school's website and take time to read all about it. A few items that you need to take note of are the following: Do they accept any high school credits? What is the yearly tuition rate? What is included/excluded in the yearly tuition rate? What is the student-to-professor ratio? What are the living requirements/dorm set up (some schools may require students to live on campus beyond freshman year)? What information do they provide about the major(s) of interest? As you research each school based on its website, be sure to take notes. Not only do you need to take notes with answers to the questions above, but you should begin to keep track of pros and cons for each school. Below I have included a basic way to keep track of information as you look at the various school websites. Create one of these charts for each school you research online that interests you.

Table 2. College Research Notes

COLLEGE NAME	
Geographic Location	
Yearly Tuition	
What is included in Tuition	
Major(s) Offered	
Professor/Student Ratio	
High School Credits	
Pros	• • •
Cons	• • •

After you have gone through each school and researched its website, you should be starting to narrow down the list of possible schools to apply to. Utilize the notes you took from each website to help determine which schools will make the final list.

If you are still struggling to narrow down your list, try ranking the notes based on your key areas. Above in Table 2 I included key areas of location, tuition, major(s), professor-to-student ratio, and whether they accept high school credits. If you have additional key areas, be sure to include those in your notes. Once you have all your key areas, rank them. Which of these choices is most aligned with what is important to you? If geographic location is one of your key areas, go through all your notes and assign a number, 1–5 (with 5 being the best geographic location you could imagine and 1 being a geographic location that you would not be a huge fan of). Repeat this process for each of the remaining areas of interest across all your notes using the 1-5 ranking technique. Then, for each college, tally up the total number based on the rankings you provided. Colleges with the highest score should illustrate selections that closely match what is important to you. From here you should be able to take the ten highest scores and have the final ten selections that you want to apply to.

As I mentioned at the beginning of this chapter, within the list of ten schools you should have two backup schools and one or two dream schools if you would like. The remaining schools are options that you would really like to attend and where you have a good chance of getting in. For most people, I would consider dream schools to be Ivy League, or any other school that you have your heart set on attending. Your backup schools should typically be in-state, public schools that offer your major(s) and would probably accept you. At this point you may be asking, how do I know if I will get in? Acceptance information should be available on the school website. Schools typically make available the percent of students accepted compared to those who applied. If a school has a 4 percent acceptance rate, that would not be a good backup school because there is a very high barrier to entry. However, if a school has a 75 percent acceptance rate, and your SAT/ACT scores align with its average acceptance figures (this should also be available on the website), this could easily be one of your backup schools.

Once you have your final list of ten, inclusive of two backup schools and one or two dream schools, the next step is simply to apply. Make sure you look at dates for when applications must be received. Not all schools have similar deadlines and you do not want to miss a deadline. Some schools even have phases for when you can apply. These can be a great benefit to you if you are ready to apply earlier than most individuals. If you apply in a later phase, the school may have already accepted a certain number of students, thereby making your pool of applicants more competitive for the remaining spots. All this information should be on the school website. If you are unable to find this information, do not hesitate to call the admissions office at any of the schools you are planning to apply to in order to clarify deadlines, whether different phases exist for applying, and if those phases can affect your chances of being accepted. Where possible, I strongly recommend applying during the earliest phase possible.

A quick side note for anyone who may already be attending a school and is considering transferring to another: make sure you understand the full implications of transferring. Does the school you want to transfer to accept transfer credits? Will it accept all the courses you have already taken? If not, how much time and money will it cost you to retake those courses at the next school? Be sure you have all information before making a decision about transferring. If you cannot find enough information on the school website, do not hesitate to call and speak to someone from the admissions office to clarify what would be transferred. You should also ask if there is any way to test out of any courses they are not willing to accept transfer credit for. Also keep transferring in mind for those of you who do not get accepted into the schools you wanted. Transfers can be a great way to switch schools after you have completed at least two semesters at the current school. Remember that your diploma will only show the school you graduated from. It will not indicate if you did not spend the entire four years there.

Last, but certainly not least, you should consider the option of online education. Online education is becoming ever more popular and accepted as a legitimate form of education. I attended an online school for my master's degree and was impressed with the level of education I received compared to my in-person undergraduate experience. The obvious pro associated with online schools is that it is cheaper (no room and board, travel, or food costs) and they offer a more flexible schedule. If you plan to work throughout school, this is a great option for you to consider. Be sure that any online school you consider is fully accredited. This information should be on the website (I will discuss accreditation later in more detail). You may also want to do research in your desired career field to see if online degrees are generally accepted.

WHERE TO APPLY CHECKLIST

✓ Limit yourself to ten applications

✓ Determine geographic locations you are willing to live in

✓ Calculate yearly travel costs

✓ Create a two-column list

✓ Select an area of study and corresponding major(s)

✓ Compile college research notes

✓ Rank selections

✓ Include two backup schools

✓ Identify application deadlines

✓ Apply in earliest phase possible

BUDGET

Now that you have decided which schools you want to apply to, one additional key factor in helping you decide which to attend remains: overall cost and budget. College is expensive. There is really no getting around this point. However, there are many colleges to choose from, some considerably less expensive than others. As you consider which college is the right fit for you, it is important to understand and truly accept how much you can really afford. This is equally important for parents to understand. I myself found it difficult to fully grasp the concept of what thousands of dollars of student loan debt translated to when I was seventeen years old and applying to several colleges at varying price ranges. Upon graduation, after receiving my first student loan bill in the mail, I quickly grasped the concept of thousands of dollars of debt.

The College Board reported that in 2012–2013 the average yearly cost for tuition, fees, and room and board was $39,518 for a private school and $17,860 for a public school.[5] That is a lot of money for one year of higher education. It is also being reported that student loans are not being repaid. A February 2013 news article points out that "students defaulted on $964 million in Perkins loans in the year ended June 2011, 20 percent more than five years earlier."[6] It is therefore critical that you take a realistic look at your budget and take the time to find a college with the area of study you are interested in that will not put you in significant student loan debt that you have no hope of repaying. And it is not only that you might not be able to repay the student loan and be in debt; there are real-world consequences when you take a student loan. The same February 2013 article states that schools such as "Yale, Penn and George Washington University have all sued former students over nonpayment."[7]

As much as you may want to attend, or send your child to, an Ivy League school, it is unrealistic for the vast majority of individuals to assume they can afford this type of education. According to the National University Rankings list on the *US News & World Report* website, tuition and fees for certain Ivy League colleges for the 2012–2013 year are as follows: Harvard University $40,866, Princeton University $38,650, and Yale University $42,300.[8] And keep in mind that these numbers are for only one year. So a four-year education based on these numbers for Ivy League would cost you $162,421.33 (based on an average of the three tuition and fees). To complicate matters, most Ivy League schools do not offer substantial scholarships, leaving the burden completely on the student and/or parent(s) (scholarships exist at these schools, but similar to other scholarships you have to qualify/apply for them, thereby indicating that they are not a guarantee). Assuming a ten-year loan term and an interest rate of 4 percent, your monthly payment would be approximately $1,644.44. That is incredibly expensive and depending on your area of study, your desired career field may not provide jobs with high enough salaries (particularly at entry level) to cover this payment, let alone additional bills such as rent or mortgage. Suffice it to say that Ivy League is unrealistic unless you have the financial fortitude to be able to afford this. Pay attention below as I outline average monthly mortgage payments to give you a comparison for how much student loan payments are.

Do not ever attend an expensive school, whether it is Ivy League or not, based on the assumption that you will get a job upon graduation that will allow you to pay that hefty student loan. My advice to you is that unless you can afford that Ivy League payment currently (whether parents will pay, you have saved up, or you have outside scholarships lined up), it is best to cross Ivy League and other super expensive schools off of your list. While this may seem like harsh advice, it is realistic. And the good news is that a great education can come from several different schools, not just Ivy League.

Nowadays I work alongside individuals who attended Ivy League, but I also work alongside individuals who attended community college. And the ironic part is that we are all in similar positions. I have seen this at several companies and organizations that I have worked both with and for, so I feel safe in generalizing this to the larger population.

Which brings me to my central argument: college is what you make it. If you take nothing else away from this book, I hope that you remember this one point. Attending

Ivy League may help you get a foot in the door, but beyond that, it is up to you to hold your own in any position you take. And there are several ways to get your foot in the door that I will discuss in further detail later in the book. And this is not to argue against Ivy League education, as they clearly provide top notch education and opportunity. This is simply to highlight that college is not about where you attend, but how hard you work wherever you choose to attend and what you make of your time there.

Knowing that Ivy League colleges are very expensive and most likely out of the realm of possibility for the vast majority of us (including myself at the time), it is important to identify what your budget range is as you move forward in selecting an appropriate school. If you have decided on your field of study and the career you would like to head into, conduct several online searches to discover the typical salary that a person in this career makes. You can conduct basic online searches using phrases such as "average nurse salary" or "accountant salary." To get more accurate and timely results, I suggest looking at online job websites such as Monster.com to tailor the results to the specific locations you are looking at.[9] Using one of these job websites, you can see what the current salary/hourly rate for a nurse would be in that geographic area. For example, you can search for nurse jobs in Denver, Colorado, or research analyst in Phoenix, Arizona. Keep these numbers handy, as they will be needed to determine how much you should spend on college. Also be sure to look at the salary/hourly rate for entry level versus more experienced positions. Immediately following college, even with internships, you will still be considered as entry level by most employers.

Therefore it is important to look at the entry-level salary range/hourly rates for this exercise, as this will be the salary you will be making when you start paying student loans.

What salary range you could make in your desired career field is very important because you do not want to overspend on your tuition for college if your career field offers a smaller salary. That would leave you with significant student loan debt and a job that does not allow you to pay off your debt in a realistic timeframe. For example, if your desired career yields a yearly salary of $30,000 in the location you want (based on your search results from above), it would be unwise to attend a college that costs $30,000 per year. This would leave you with $120,000 in student loan debt over your four-year education that you would have to start paying shortly after graduation (several student loans offer you a several-month grace period after college graduation before your first payment is due). Your average monthly payment would be about $1,272.79 at a 5 percent interest rate on a ten-year loan. That is simply far too much to feasibly pay on a $30,000 salary when you look at other expenses such as rent/mortgage and food. To put this amount in perspective, a 2012 article sourcing information collected by LendingTree reported that the most expensive average monthly mortgage payment (per state) in the United States for the time frame of November 2011 to November 2012 was in Washington, DC, at $1,641 per month.[10]

I recommend that you take time to research salaries online to determine what you will be able to afford upon graduation. In addition to looking at current job openings in your desired location to determine salary, I also recommend looking at websites like studentsreviews.com/salary_by_major. This website will highlight both entry-level salaries and current salaries by individuals who majored in a variety of areas.[11] I would recommend cross-referencing information you receive from several websites to draw a more balanced conclusion.

Once you can gauge the salary you can expect for your desired career field at entry level and beyond, you still need to understand your budget after graduation and how much the essentials will cost you (which include your student loan debt). To accomplish this you will need to create a spreadsheet. Each individual may have different expenses. I have included below a basic approach to help you determine whether your student loan debt will be at an acceptable level based on potential income for your desired career field. At the bare minimum, you will need to include in your budget rent, food, gasoline (substitute public transportation if you plan to use this in place of your own vehicle), car payment (if applicable), cell phone (I consider this a necessity in case of emergency), gas, electric, and water. Feel free to include additional line items if needed or replace line items in my example below with line items that apply to you.

Table 3. Example of Budget Spreadsheet

MONTHLY EXPENSES	AMOUNT	PERCENT
Rent	$ 800.00	26.7%
Food	$ 200.00	6.7%
Gasoline	$ 100.00	3.3%
Car Insurance	$ 62.80	2.1%
Toiletries/Dry Clean	$ 125.00	4.2%
Cable	$ 69.00	2.3%
Cell Phone	$ 68.00	2.3%
Electric	$ 40.00	1.3%
Gas	$ 29.00	1.0%
Water	$ 18.00	0.6%
Hair/Makeup	$ 55.00	1.8%
Pet	$ 75.00	2.5%
Student Loan	$ 250.00	8.3%
Total Expenses	$ 1,891.80	63.1%
Income	$ 3,000.00	
Excess	$ 1,108.20	36.9%

If you are unsure of what additional line items might apply to you, talk to your parents or adult relatives and friends. Once you have all the line items for what your expenses would be after graduation, you need to start inputting approximate numbers for what each line item will cost on a monthly basis. To calculate rent I recommend conducting research online at one of the apartment renting websites such as Apartments.com or looking at rentals on Craigslist in the geographical areas of interest.[12,13] Several websites, such as bankrate.com also offer cost-of-living calculators to help you derive approximate numbers for the remaining line items such as water, energy, and food bills.[14] Be sure to also include what your monthly income would be based on your earlier salary research for entry-level positions. This will require additional steps to determine federal and state income taxes depending on the salary range. For example, if your estimated entry-level salary for your desired career field will be $30,000, determine which federal tax bracket you would fall within using the IRS.gov website and what your state income tax would be using individual state government websites.[15] Also deduct social security taxes, details of which can also be found on the IRS website.[16] In sum, take your estimated salary and subtract yearly federal and state income taxes and social security taxes (depending on additional factors, other items may apply that would reduce your take-home pay). Next, divide this number by twelve to arrive at your approximate monthly income. Total expenses should be the sum of all the line items above it. Excess should be Income minus Total Expenses. If your excess is a negative number, you would be losing money each month and therefore something needs to change, such as the amount you pay for student loan debt (thereby indicating you would need to reduce the amount you take out in student loans). If your excess is barely above zero you may want to look at changing something because chances are you will want additional money each month to put toward retirement, a savings account, going out on weekends, etc.

Above I did not include savings as a mandatory line item under expenses. I strongly recommend that you try to save as much as possible per month for a savings account and retirement. When you are just starting out, that is the best time to save because your money will have several decades to compound interest, thereby increasing the overall amount you will have. It is also important to have money set aside in savings in case anything occurs that you weren't planning for such as a major illness or if you were to lose your job due to budget cuts. I understand that it is difficult to find money to save, particularly when you are starting out, but again this will greatly benefit you in the long run. Even if you are only able to save $50 per month, that will still allow you to build up savings over time. Every little bit counts, so be sure to set aside something each month for savings. Plan ahead and be prepared for the unexpected when it comes to your money.

Additionally, you can add a percentage column as I have done in Table 3. For example, the percentage column for rent would be your rent number divided by monthly income. Some people find it easier to look at percentages. Either way you choose to look at it (numbers versus percentages), your income number needs to be greater than your overall expenses. When using this spreadsheet you should be able to see what amount you could realistically spend on a student loan payment each month in combination with other bills. You can easily accomplish this by inserting all other monthly expenses first and leaving the student loan payment at zero. Try plugging in different numbers such as 150, 250, etc. and watch how that will affect your monthly expenses and what you will have in excess. Any number for the student loan payment that causes excess to be a negative number is too expensive, and you therefore cannot afford that student loan payment.

If you haven't done so already, you will need to calculate the range of possibilities for what your monthly student loan payment would be, based on the colleges you researched earlier (the above numbers you plugged in were examples to get you started). In order to do this, you will need to pull out your College Research Notes as explained in the previous chapter. In these notes you wrote down the basic tuition and fees for several colleges. You should now go further in depth on each college you applied to/were accepted to and determine a more accurate cost to attend. In addition to tuition and fees there are other expenses that you may need to pay for. Here is a table that you will need to fill out for each college.

Table 4. College Costs

	Application Fee	Tuition and Fees	Room and Board*	Food*	Travel	Totals
1						
2						
3						
4						
5						
6						
7						
8						
9						
10						

*These items may be included in tuition and fees

Once you have the totals for each of the colleges, you will need to take that number multiplied by four (to account for a typical four-year undergraduate education) and then use any of the several online calculators to provide you with information on what your monthly payment would be. Examples of these websites include bankrate. com and finaid.org.[17,18] Calculate what your monthly payment would be for each school. Be sure to use a timely and accurate interest rate (average rates being offered can also be researched online) and plan for no more than a ten-year loan term. To better understand the interest rate you might qualify for, consider asking a local banker.

You should now have ten different monthly payments that you can apply to your budget spreadsheet to determine whether your student loan payment would be feasible based on your desired career field and entry-level salary. If all your colleges have payments that would be too expensive upon graduation, don't worry, as you can work to acquire scholarships to assist.

I also want to make quick note of additional expenses you will incur throughout college, which will include books, supplies, and extra money (you will still need to buy clothes, eat out/purchase groceries, and spend some money on entertainment). For the purposes of this book, I am assuming that these costs will be relatively the same no matter which college you choose; therefore, I have not included them as determining factors in Table 4. You should absolutely buy used books only and you can sell them back when you are done with the course at a reduced price, assuming you don't need that book for a follow-on course. I would recommend that you check your college bookstore for used books as well as online vendors such as Half.com.[19]

Scholarships can significantly reduce the total cost of any college you want to attend, as scholarships are money that does not need to be repaid (because scholarships are money given to you there may be tax implications so be sure to check with a financial or tax accountant). Some schools offer scholarships through the school and others are offered independent of any school affiliation. Within the subset of schools that offer scholarships, you may have to apply separately for these scholarships while some colleges will consider your basic college application as the application for the scholarships as well. This information should be available on their website. If you are unable to find scholarship information online for any one school, be sure to call and verify. As mentioned above, in addition to scholarships offered by individual schools, there are numerous scholarships offered independent of schools. These can range from nominal amounts, such as $500, all the way up to thousands of dollars in scholarship money. My recommendation to you is to apply to as many scholarships as possible, even if they are in a smaller amount. Smaller amounts can add up quickly, and for every dollar you get via scholarship, that is one less dollar (and interest) you have to pay back upon graduation. In my experience, most individuals choose to apply only to the larger amount scholarships, which significantly reduces the competition for the smaller amount scholarships. There is plenty of scholarship money available; you simply have to be willing to take the time to apply for each scholarship individually. There are several websites that help locate available scholarships. Examples of some of these websites include: scholarships.com, fastweb.com, and finaid.org.[20,21,22] Your goal should be to go to college for free. Similar to applying to colleges, don't assume that you can apply to one and be done. Apply for several scholarships and assume that you will not get them all. I recommend that you begin applying for scholarships as soon as you finish applications for your ten colleges. Also remember that scholarships have deadlines for applying, so be sure to pay close attention to deadlines to provide yourself enough time to prepare your applications.

If you are having trouble attaining scholarships and will be unable to pay for your college education, consider serving in the United States military. There are typically two common options here: join a Reserve Officers' Training Corps (ROTC) program, which will allow you to attend college immediately following high school with an agreement to serve in the military upon graduation, or enlist in the military and receive the benefits, which may include assistance for education either during your military tenure or after.[23] If you are interested in either of these options remember that signing a military contract is binding and should not be taken lightly. Also be sure to discuss what tuition assistance would be applicable to you before you sign any contracts. On the other hand, joining the military is a great way to build real-life experience that can be translated to job experience, particularly since the military will train you in your specific area at no additional charge to you. If you decide that you are interested in this option, I would recommend researching the various US military branches online (e.g., Marines, Air Force, Army, Navy, Coast Guard) and talk to friends/relatives who chose to pursue this route.[24,25,26,27,28] They should be able to give you the pros and cons of this decision.

At this point, if you still require loans to pay for your education, I recommend that you do in-depth research on the types of student loans available that you qualify for. I would also recommend that you look for college options within your area of study that might be completely free of charge. A January 2013 news article suggests that there are at least a few "tuition-free or tuition-reduced" schools.[29] While the specific schools listed in this article may not apply to you based on your area of study and geographical preferences, the important takeaway is that there are several ways to reduce the cost of college. However, you must do research and put in the time and effort toward obtaining scholarships or reduced-fee options. A recent article even suggests that some states, such as Texas, Florida, and Wisconsin, may attempt to offer $10,000 bachelor degrees in the future.[30]

Student loans are extremely common these days, but I want to impress on you the seriousness of taking out student loans. In a November 2012 press release, the Federal Reserve Bank of New York stated that "outstanding student loan debt now stands at $956 billion, an increase of $42 billion since last quarter," and that "the percent of student loan balances 90+ days delinquent increased to 11 percent this quarter."[31] While these types of loans are prevalent, it is also important to highlight that the delinquent (behind on payments) percentage is very high. This should be a forewarning to you that you should take out student loans only for an amount that you are absolutely certain you will be able to repay, which is why figuring out your budget based on desired career is a critical step to complete. Failure to repay your student loans will affect your credit score, which you will need to obtain loans for everything from cars to houses in the future. Also, depending on how long your payments are delinquent you may be required to pay additional fees, which will increase the overall amount you owe (different loans will have different rules on delinquency and fees you may incur, so be sure you understand what the consequences would be if you fall behind on payments).

There are several types of student loans available. At the basic overview level, student loans can be broken into two categories: private and non-private. Private student loans are offered through private entities such as banks. Non-private student loans are typically federal (or federally sponsored) student loans. According to the Federal Student Aid government website there are four major categories of federal student loans: direct subsidized loans, direct unsubsidized loans, direct PLUS loans, and direct consolidation loans.[32] Which of these federal student loans you qualify for depends on your individual financial needs. To help you determine which you qualify for, you need to fill out the Free Application for Federal Student Aid (FAFSA), which is available at http://www.fafsa.ed.gov/.[33] Also keep in mind that there are limits to how much you can borrow, so do not expect student loans to cover the entire cost of your college. As I mentioned earlier, your goal should be to go to college for free by obtaining enough scholarships. Student loans are a last resort if you are unable to obtain enough scholarships. Another common type of student loan is the Federal Perkins Loan Program, which is "a school-based loan program for undergraduates and graduate students with exceptional financial need. Under this program, the school is lender," compared to the previously described federal loans where the lender is the US Department of Education.[34]

The Federal Aid Student Loan website also states that in particular teacher and public service situations student loans may be forgiven, meaning that you do not have to pay back the loan(s).[35] Certain restrictions apply, however, so if these are career paths of interest to you be sure to understand the restrictions and whether this will apply to you.

Grants are another type of assistance that you can apply for via the FAFSA. The US Department of Education also offers four types of grants that are similar to scholarships in that they do not need to be repaid: Federal Pell Grants, Federal Supplemental Educational Opportunity Grants (FSEOG), Teacher Education Assistance for College and Higher Education (TEACH) Grants, and Iraq and Afghanistan Service Grants.[36]

As I mentioned above, private student loans are also available. When you are ready to apply for student loans, you need to do in-depth research on each loan to determine your best option(s). Questions you need to research for each loan include: What is the interest rate? Over how many years is repayment? Is there a grace period and, if so, how long? What are the repercussions of delayed payments? Clearly you want to find a student loan with a low interest rate and a realistic time frame for repayment (you probably do not want to be repaying your student loan thirty years down the road). Ideally, you also want to find a student loan that offers a grace period—a short time frame after graduation before you have to start making payments.

No matter which student loan(s) you decide on, be absolutely sure you understand the fine print. Student loans are binding contracts and you will be held liable. Furthermore, the Federal Aid Student Loan website states that only in "rare cases" can a student loan be discharged in bankruptcy, so your student loan will stick with you year after year until you repay it.[37]

You need to be realistic with the college you choose. Keep it affordable, and you will thank yourself in later years.

BUDGET CHECKLIST

✓ Realize and accept how much you can truly afford

✓ Do not attend an expensive school on the assumption you will get a job to cover the cost

✓ Remember that college is less about where you attend, and more about what you make of your time where you attend

✓ Determine desired career entry salary

✓ Derive monthly budget based on salary (including student loan payments)

✓ Calculate college affordability based on monthly student loan payment

✓ Apply for scholarships

✓ Consider other options to reduce college expenses

✓ Apply for student loans and grants

FRESHMAN YEAR, LOOKING AHEAD

Once you have decided on which college to attend based on your applications and acceptances, the next step in making college count is freshman year. In my experience, most students view freshman year as the time to define their independence, enjoy the freedom and responsibility of being an adult, and take easy courses while they determine what they want to do with their life. I couldn't disagree more. Freshman year is your time to get ahead, make connections, and focus on your academics. I was one of few students at my college who knew what they wanted to major in and did not change it before graduation. In fact, I ended up having enough time to add a second major, which helped make me more marketable when it came time to apply for internships and ultimately interview for full-time positions.

Before you start courses freshman year, you should receive a course handbook from the college. This book may be titled something different, but it will be a detailed guide outlining the available majors and minors, and the requirements for each major/minor in order to graduate. You need to read this book front to back and become intimately familiar with it. This book is your key to shortcuts and success. Contained within this book are several ways to create shortcuts for yourself, depending on the major(s) you select. For example, most colleges have a standard set of core courses that you must complete. This typically will include courses on writing, research, computer basics, etc. And, lest we forget, the ever favorite physical education credit(s). A common mistake is for freshman to take all the easy courses, such as physical education, during their first or second semester. While this may seem like a good idea at the time, once you are taking all your difficult courses at the same time during later semesters, you will regret this decision. Toward the end of your time at college you will also want to be focusing on internships, which will be time intensive. The ability to fall back on some of those easy courses at that time will be a lifesaver. During my final semesters, I took ballroom dancing to fulfill my physical education credits. Having an easy course mixed in with my difficult, higher-level courses required for my majors allowed me to focus on those courses and excel in my academics, which in turn made me more marketable to employers.

In addition to mixing the easy courses with the more difficult ones, a very important way you can create a shortcut for yourself is to use the core curriculum to satisfy major and minor requirements as well. I will explain this point from my own experience. As a freshman, I knew I wanted to major in political science. So I pulled out the course handbook and identified which courses were required for this major. I then cross-referenced this list with the core curriculum required courses. And sure enough, there were courses that appeared in both. Thus, I was able to take one course that satisfied my core curriculum as well as got me one course closer to my major.

The only assumption here is that as a freshman you know what you want to major in. And while I understand that things change over time, it is crucial that you plan ahead and decide on at least one major that you plan to follow through on. Unless the major you change to is very close to the one you were already working on, this change will adversely affect you, directly resulting in more semesters at school, which equates to more money you may owe in student loans. At this point you should have a good idea of what you want to major in based on earlier chapters. If you were unable to select a college based on area of study, re-read the previous chapters to assist you in selecting a major.

Remember, you are on a mission. Your fellow students, particularly the students sharing the same majors and minors as you, are your competition. They will be the ones fighting for the same internships and full-time positions. Getting a head start freshman year is an important step in making yourself more marketable and separating yourself from the competition. Knowing your major from day one is one of the best decisions you can make to get a head start.

A quick side note about signing up for courses, particularly during your freshman year: the majority of courses (depending on the size of your school and professor-to-student ratio) have a limited number of spots and will fill up quickly. Be sure that you are ready to sign up within the earliest time frame allowable. Different schools have different rules about how they determine who gets to sign up first, so be prepared; as a freshman you may be at the bottom of the list and may not get your top choices. Do not wait until it is time to actually sign up for courses to start researching which courses you should take. This should be done well in advance. I recommend that you have multiple options laid out to sign up for, all of which still satisfy your major and core curriculum requirements. If, despite your best efforts, the courses fill up and you are left with options that serve you no purpose, I recommend you meet directly with each professor. Oftentimes they will be willing to make an exception and override the typical number of seats available. Also, students at most colleges are allowed to drop/add classes within the first few weeks without penalty. This may give you an opportunity to add a previously filled class. As mentioned before, when you meet with the professor(s) you need to be prepared and have a detailed explanation of why you should be let into this course.

Once you know your major and have had a few weeks to become familiar with the college, you need to start the process of identifying your academic adviser. At some schools, the advisers are not the professors. When I speak of academic advisers, I am indicating the scenarios where the academic advisers are the professors. If you are at a college where the professors are not the official advisers, you will still need to identify at least one professor that will become your unofficial adviser. This person will help guide you in course selection(s) throughout your time at college as well as help you find and apply to internships and full-time positions upon graduation.

In selecting the right professor, first talk to other students, particularly the older students in your major courses that have been at the college for at least a few semesters. They should have a good gauge on which professors are active in their respective fields (technically they all should be; however, some may be more active than others) and which are known to assist students in obtaining internships and ultimately jobs. Active in their field typically indicates that professors are conducting research and publishing on relevant topics. Suffice it to say that professors are an excellent way to network within your desired career field. More importantly, some colleges place limits on how many students each professor can advise. By approaching them during your freshman year, you are getting your foot in the door, assuming that they may not have room to add you now (some schools may also have restrictions on declaring a major during your first semester and selecting an adviser early on so you want to be prepared as soon as you are able to declare a major and identify an adviser). You are also showing your determination and drive, attributes that professors are bound to notice.

If you are at a small college, this will be much easier than those of you at large or online colleges where hundreds of students might attend each class. The best way to start this process, once you have identified the possible professors you would like to advise you, is to request a meeting to discuss with them in person. Professors are customarily required to have a certain number of office hours, so this is as simple as stopping by (or calling) the department office and setting up an appointment. If you attend an online college,

I would recommend sending an e-mail to the professors to get the process started.

Another shortcut you can take advantage of from your course handbook is the ability to add a second major at a low cost. Several majors are closely related to one another. In the same way that core curriculum offerings will overlap with majors, several courses will satisfy more than one major course requirement. Therefore, if you select two majors that are at least somewhat related to one another, there is a good chance that by taking one course you can satisfy requirements for both. This is important for several reasons. Most importantly, having a double major is another way you can set yourself apart from the competition when it comes to internships and full-time positions. In my opinion, double majors indicate the ability to multitask, a critical skill set required of any field. This is also another bullet point to add to your resume. Resumes are critical to getting your foot in the door at internships and full-time positions, so anything you can add is important (I will discuss resumes in more detail later in the book).

For example, in addition to political science, I was able to add an international studies major. The two are related closely enough that I was able to make several courses satisfy requirements for both majors, and yet different enough that employers appreciate the additional knowledge base my second major provides.

Don't overlook another critical shortcut that you can take advantage of before college. Several high schools offer classes that can result in college credit. These classes typically require you to take a test at the end, and based on your test results you can receive varying amounts of college credit. The most common of these classes stem from the Advanced Placement classes, more commonly referred to as AP courses.[38] High school students can choose to take one or many AP courses depending on their interests. There are thirty-four different AP courses to choose from, however all thirty-four may not be offered at each high school.[39] Typically only the higher scores will result in college credit, so it is important to take these classes seriously and study for the tests. The AP exams cost $89 each, and while this may seem like a decent amount of money, in comparison, it is only a fraction of the cost that a college would charge you for an equivalent course.[40] If you are able to take AP courses, I highly encourage it, as you will save yourself significant time and money by the time you enter college. AP courses are a great way to satisfy those core curriculum requirements such as math and science.

In addition to AP, some high schools offer the International Baccalaureate (IB) Program.[41] Similar to AP, the key difference is that students who enter the IB Program are required to take advanced courses in all subjects, whereas AP allows students to select as many subjects as they are comfortable with. The IB Program is also a globally recognized program, so if you are considering attending a college outside the United States, this may be an important point to consider. IB Programs are less commonly found in high schools, so it is important to research what is available at your high school and look into additional options within your school district if necessary. IB exams may also cost money to take, so be sure to check with your high school regarding what fees are required.

If you are planning to take AP or IB courses, or already have taken them, it is important to note that not all colleges accept the AP or IB test scores as college credit. Based on my personal research, public colleges tend to grant more credit than private colleges. When determining where to apply, this is an important factor to consider. For example, I attended a private college that was not willing to grant the same level of credits that public in-state schools offered. My younger sister attended an in-state public college and was able to acquire significantly more college credits, nearly walking in the door as a sophomore on her first day of college. I was granted twenty-one credits based on my high school work (an average two-semester course load is thirty credits). This information is typically available on the college's website. If not, don't hesitate to contact the admissions office and request further information about receiving college credit for AP and/or IB courses.

If the college you have decided on does not recognize all the courses you took in high school, you still have options. You can contact the head of each department and ask if there are other options to test out of any of the courses based on the work you completed in high school. For example, I scored a 6 out of 7 on the IB calculus test but my college did not officially recognize this and was not willing to give me the credit up front. I needed a math course to satisfy my core curriculum requirements and I was determined not to waste my time taking a course that I had already taken, and tested very well on, in high school. So I contacted one of the professors from the appropriate department and illustrated the work I had completed. I then had to prove that I completed work at the level required in the college's course and ultimately was granted the credit. Admittedly, this took a fair amount of diplomatic negotiation on my end to prove my high school work. But it saved me from having to take a course I had already taken, which also saved me money and allowed me to take other courses.

For those of you currently in the working world that are thinking about going back to school, you may be able to translate some of your working experience or training into college credit. Most colleges will advertise this openly so be sure to research this online and determine how many credits you can receive. Every little bit counts. Even if it is only one class that you will receive credit for, that is one less class you have to pay for and take time out of your busy schedule to complete. It will behoove you to do this research up front.

All these shortcuts add up to another critical point: the possibility of graduating early. This is important, even if you graduate only one semester early. If you are able to graduate in December, you will be entering the working world at a time when most of your competition (other students) is still in school. Essentially, you are making yourself more marketable simply by the fact that there are fewer college applicants at this point in time. I graduated in December, one semester ahead of the rest of my class and officially started work as a full-time employee on January 5, a mere sixteen days after graduation. Looking back I would have loved to have had some time off to enjoy, but several of my friends who did this and were not aggressive in obtaining a job straight out of college are still without jobs. The good news is that once employed you should have vacation or paid time off, and vacation is much sweeter when your time off is paid for by your company and you know that you have a job to sustain your lifestyle and pay the bills.

Another reason you may want to consider graduating early is if you are on a full or partial scholarship. Some schools may let you apply that scholarship funding toward an advanced, or graduate degree, so long as it is within the first four years and you obtain the advanced degree at the same school. This may apply particularly if you are working on a joint/combination program whereby a college offers both a bachelor's and master's degree over a shorter time than if you were to pursue each degree separately. Be sure to research this ahead of time and get definitive answers. Don't join a combined degree program or make decisions on the assumption that scholarship money will transfer over.

My advice to you is to be your own advocate and don't be afraid to ask for these things. I would not assume that a college would advertise this information in all instances, but they may be willing to accommodate you if you present them with a valid and diplomatic argument. In the same way that I had to fight for my calculus credit when it was not advertised as college credit, you must also look for ways to create shortcuts for yourself. Every little bit helps and can create opportunity for you at each turn.

FRESHMAN YEAR CHECKLIST

✓ Freshman year is your time to get ahead

✓ Utilize course handbook to take advantage of shortcuts among course requirements

✓ Register for courses as early as possible and have backup courses ready

✓ Do not take all your easy courses freshman year

✓ Identify academic adviser

✓ Consider a second major

✓ Obtain college credit for high school courses (AP/IB)

INTERNSHIPS

Now that you have survived freshman year and declared your major, it is important to start looking for internships. Internships are short-term jobs that are related to your desired career field that will provide training and experience to assist you in landing a full-time position. While it is never too early to start, I recommend that you obtain your first internship the summer after your sophomore year at college. You should then obtain a second internship between your junior and senior years of college. You need to have at least two internships completed before graduation. This will help establish you as a serious contender for jobs, allow you to add substance to your resume, and help you stand out among other students also applying for full-time positions as your college education draws to an end. Internships are critical because they provide real-world experience. This is the difference between theoretical and practical experience; college should provide you the theoretical experience of how things should work, and internships provide you the real-world application of what you learned in college. An important note here is that real-world application is often strikingly different than what you learn in college. So again, internships are critical in highlighting the fact that you can take theory (what you learned in college) and translate it to the real world. That is what an employer is looking for in potential hires.

Successful internships are the key to landing your first full-time position after college. Oftentimes, assuming that you do well at your internship, internships themselves will result in a contingent job offer. This happened to me, and I ended up accepting the full-time job offer from my second internship. I will also note that I left my first internship with a part-time position while I was still in school as well. Internships are an excellent way to get your foot in the door and start making connections within your desired field.

A second, equally important aspect to internships is the concept of networking. Think of networking as your extended network of professional friends. Put more simply, networking is all about who you know. In my personal experience I have found that networking is absolutely critical in getting your foot in the door for any position. Through internships you are introducing yourself to a new professional network of colleagues, who, in turn, are connected to additional professional colleagues both internal to their own company and likely other companies as well. A January 2013 *New York Times* news article maintained that "even getting in the door for an interview is becoming more difficult for those without connections. Referred candidates are twice as likely to land an interview as other applicants, according to a new study of one large company by three economists from the Federal Reserve Bank of New York. For those who make it to the interview stage, the referred candidates had a 40 percent better chance of being hired than other applicants."[42] This same article further stipulates that "big companies like Ernst & Young are increasingly using their own workers to find new hires, saving time and money but lengthening the odds for job seekers without connections, especially among the long-term unemployed."[43] This article highlights the same points I mentioned above: having a network of professionals in your field is critical to landing a job. While in college, the most logical way to begin your network is through internships.

Now that you understand how critical internships are to long-term success, it is also important to note how difficult it is to land your first internship. At this point you most likely have little to no practical experience in your field, and convincing an employer that you are the right person for the internship is no easy feat. You must be willing to accept rejections, and hedge these rejections by applying to several internships. Also be willing to accept that you will most likely not get paid for your first internship. It is not uncommon that internships are not paid or pay very little. And while this will result in a financial setback, internships are still the right decision long term because it will give you a competitive advantage for a full-time position after graduation. My first internship paid only a small monthly stipend, which was not enough to cover my rent, but in the long term, this internship proved critical in securing my follow-on internship the next summer and ultimately my first full-time position.

I want to make a quick side note about the possibility of a financial setback in order to take your first internship. If you can get a well-compensated first internship, that is great. For everyone else, be sure you run the numbers and can actually afford the financial setback. I had to live off savings during my first summer internship and had to significantly cut back on the nonessentials. That same summer I also had the option to do a summer abroad in Spain not only to study but for an internship as well. This option would have cost me significantly more and was an option I was unable to afford at the time. The important point here is that I was mature enough to make the right financial decision at the time. Similar to college, as long as the internship is somehow related to your desired career field, it is less about where and what the internship is, and more about what you accomplish with your time at the internship. Be sure to apply to several internships so that you have options to choose from. You should never take out an additional loan in order to fulfill an internship. If you are unable to afford an internship you should look at working part-time somewhere else in addition to your internship. Both summers of my internships I looked at the possibility of additional part-time work to help cover costs.

My advice to you during internships is to buckle down and put in the long hours. This is a critical time in your career, as you are just making a name for yourself.

Most internships occur during the summer, and this is when competition is at its peak. Research internships available during the school year as a backup option should you have trouble obtaining summer internships. Most schools will let you use an internship related to your major for college credit (college credit may preclude you from getting paid for that specific internship); however, this would most likely indicate that the internship would be part-time for a semester while you are simultaneously taking classes.

Where possible, I recommend summer internships that are full-time because it allows you to truly become an employee for a short period of time. You will get a better idea of the workplace environment at this company (remember, you may get a job offer out of the internship and want to truly understand what working here full-time would be like). You are also more likely to be asked to take on more important duties and assignments when you are on site forty hours per week and able to constantly work (employers may be resistant to providing you with important assignments if they know you are splitting your time between school and the internship).

If you are having trouble getting your first internship you should also look at full-time internships during the fall or spring. This would indicate that you would have to switch around a semester of school and possibly make up courses during the summer or winter break. Schools will have varying schedules over the summer and winter breaks so be cognizant of any restraints before accepting a full-time internship during the typical school year. If you choose this path I advise that you do not simply take the semester off altogether, as this will cause you to graduate a semester later. As important as summers and time off from school may be to you, having a full-time position upon graduation is more important.

Whether you are doing a part-time or full-time internship, it is important to remember that you must perform well at this internship if you want to obtain a job offer or use the employer as a reference in the future. This goes back to my previous comment that you are on a mission. Be willing to work extra hours for free (I know this may be difficult to muster now, but remember, this will pay off in the long run) and always volunteer to help out with extra duties. I also recommend that during each internship you select one person to act as your adviser throughout your internship. Some companies may do this through a mentor program, but you will need to initiate this process for those that don't. This should be a person that you feel comfortable working with and asking questions. Use this person as a sounding board for questions about the career field and ways you can continue to work toward this career field while still in college.

Another equally important reason that you need to impress during your internships is networking, as I mentioned above. I am continually surprised at what a small world it seems to be. I constantly run into individuals from my old jobs. You never know who is connected to whom. If you burn a bridge at your internship that could very well preclude you from obtaining follow-on internships or positions at a variety of companies. This is your one chance to make a great first impression in your desired career field, so make it a good one.

If you find that you enjoyed the internship and the work you were able to perform, be sure to ask about follow-on opportunities before you go. Before I left my first internship to head back to school, I requested a meeting with the director (I interned at a nonprofit organization in Washington, DC) and asked if they would be willing to hire me part-time throughout the fall while I went back to college. I came prepared to the meeting with details on what work I could perform and why it would be beneficial to the organization to keep me on. I walked out of the meeting with a part-time paying job. Those few short months of hard work had already paid off.

This part-time job was difficult for me to keep with my college schedule, and I ended up having to quit early that fall to focus on my academics (full-time college and a DC job proved difficult to juggle), but both of those experiences helped me land my next internship the following summer. The first internship is the hardest to land. From there, it should be much easier.

Chances are if you are applying for internships, you have a good idea of where you want to apply. If you are not sure, this would be a great time to engage your academic advisers and/or ask fellow students (typically those that are a year or two ahead of you) about internship opportunities. This should yield a few options, but chances are these options have also been told to other students (also known as your competition). So it is important again to note that you should apply to multiple internships. Do not ever assume that you will get an internship, particularly if this is your first hopeful internship. I would apply to at least ten internships your first time. Thankfully, applying to internships is typically free and will only cost you time and effort.

When applying for internships, think outside the box. Don't just apply to the obvious internships for your desired career path. Apply to anywhere that would yield the skill sets required for your desired career field. For example, if you want to be a research analyst, applying to newspapers, magazines, and nonprofit organizations are all great ideas. Each of these would require you to learn the process of researching and writing, which are essential skills for a research analyst. If you are unsure of what skill sets are required, look at any of the online job websites at active positions companies are trying to fill. Most should list required qualifications or skill sets. Once you know what skill sets you must acquire, look online for several internship options. You can use any of the various job websites and search by the term intern or internship. You can also utilize your college's career/job office as well (not all colleges will have this). Additional websites exist to help you learn about and identify internships such as internmatch.com, college.monster.com/education, and internships.about.com.[44, 45, 46]

If you are still unable to obtain an internship, don't stop trying. Talk to the professors at your college. Most of them are active in their field, and would be more than happy to have free help. One of my professors had a grant to conduct research for a topic she was working on at the time. She let me and a few other students assist her in the research portion. It was a great way to add experience to my resume, which ultimately helped me land internships.

Another important item with internships is the timing of when you should apply. Not unlike applying for jobs upon college graduation, if you start looking for internships in April and plan to start in May or June, you are too late. You should begin researching internships during September for a summer internship the following year. Many internships will only accept applications for the summer term up until January or February of that year. Therefore you need to start looking several months in advance to ensure that you will not miss any cutoff dates.

Once you have applied to several internships, follow up. After two weeks of applying, if you have not received a response, I recommend e-mailing or calling. Be sure to be diplomatic and convey your sincere interest in the position. Assuming you receive an e-mail response, which you should, or are able to speak to the correct person on the phone, you have now made contact and again set yourself apart from the competition. Following up highlights your interest in the position more than simply sending in an application. Depending on the initial response you receive from this first follow-up, you may want to follow up one more time a few weeks down the road. I recommend limiting yourself to only two follow-ups throughout the application/interview process for an internship. This is enough to convey your interest, but not too much to signify neediness.

Once you have completed your first internship, you should have a better understanding of your desired career field and what your next internship should look like. I recommend that you do not intern with the same company and have that count as your two internships. If this is the only option, then yes, you should accept it as your second internship. However, I highly recommend that you intern with a different company for your second internship for two reasons. The first is networking. By working for a different company within the same career field, you are introducing yourself to an entirely new set of individuals whom you can utilize as mentors and advisers. This may also assist you in the long run. Having a lengthy network is extremely helpful if you are trying to find a full-time position. The more people you can reach out to, the greater the chance you will land an interview. The second reason is skill sets. You want to garner as much experience as possible between these two internships before you enter the working world full-time. If you work at the same (or similar) company two years in a row, you may be limiting yourself to the types of skill sets you can gain experience in.

At both internships, ask one of your colleagues/mentors to assist you in the write-up for your resume. They will be more familiar with the key words associated with this career field that employers will look for in resumes.

INTERNSHIPS CHECKLIST

✓ Internships are critical to landing a full-time job after graduation

✓ You need two internships throughout college

✓ Internships are your introduction to networking

✓ Acquiring your first internship will be very difficult

✓ Accept that you will most likely not get paid for your first internship

✓ Opt for full-time internships

✓ Put in the long hours; internships are your only chance to make a professional impression during college

✓ Internships can lead to job offers at the company you intern for if you excel at your internship

✓ Apply for several internships very early on; assume you will get rejected on most applications

✓ Identify mentors/advisers at each of your internships

MAKING YOURSELF
MARKETABLE

In each of the previous chapters, I have outlined several ways to help you get a few steps ahead throughout college with the ultimate goal of graduating with a job in your desired career field. A significant part of obtaining your desired job is making yourself marketable, not only to set yourself apart from the competition, but to further enhance your view from an employer perspective. You want employers to see you as an excellent bet, someone who will excel in the position, and create business for the company. Internships, as discussed in the previous chapter, are the first step in making yourself marketable.

In addition to excelling at two (or more) internships, you should also strive to find ways to make yourself more marketable through your course work. This can be achieved in several ways: papers that you write for school, special courses not always offered, independent studies, and foreign languages. While most students write papers with only the end of the semester in mind, you are on a mission and should be thinking about these papers as possible line items on your resume. I myself have a line item on my resume for related coursework where I list specific courses I have taken throughout my education that align with sought-after skill sets in my career field. Under this section in your resume, not only can you list specific courses, but you can include any papers that relate to your career field that would help make you more marketable. For example, if you are hoping to land in a marketing career and wrote a paper on innovative marketing techniques for small companies utilizing the latest technology trends, you should absolutely include that on your resume. In addition to your resume, be sure to mention relevant course work and papers during any interviews. I would even recommend that you bring a copy with you to interviews, and if prospective employers seem interested, offer them a copy. This shows that even during college you were interested in this career field and have already begun thinking about ways to increase efficiency and prospective business for that company. These are absolutely desired qualities that an employer is looking for in prospective employees, whether they are intern positions or full-time positions. With this being said, be sure that this is a great paper you wrote during college. Don't offer a paper that you received a low grade on because there were spelling errors and you didn't explain your argument well. A paper can work against you as well as for you, so be sure to select appropriate papers for inclusion in your resume and at interviews.

Special courses are another great way to make yourself more marketable. This will require your course handbook that I mentioned earlier. Remember, after you begin to sign up for your first semester of courses in college you quickly learn that not all courses listed are offered at all times, and even if they are offered they may fill up before you can register. Often, courses are offered every other semester or even every few years. While frustrating, this illustrates that planning ahead is essential to taking the courses you need. Based on your declared major(s), look through the course handbook and identify courses based on the descriptions provided that relate to your desired career field. Ideally, you should be able to find courses that not only interest you, but will also make you more marketable based on the content as it relates to the career field. Once you have identified a few of these courses, ensure that they will satisfy requirements for graduation. For example, if you find two courses that you want to take, but you need only one course from that category for graduation, see if you can find another course from a separate category that will serve the same purpose. If you are unsure of which courses you need from which categories, be sure to schedule a meeting with your academic adviser before making any final decisions. If you take two courses and only one will count toward your graduation/ major requirements, you are wasting time and money. If, on the other hand, you have your heart set on both courses, talk to your academic adviser about substituting one of them as an elective course. This may require you to get signatures from the department or other decision makers, so be prepared to present your argument; this is similar to negotiating for college credit for AP and IB courses taken in high school.

Going back to the discussion on selecting courses that directly correlate to your desired career field, if you are unable to find at least two courses that would directly benefit your attempts to get to your desired career field, I recommend you try for an independent study course. Most majors should have this listed as an option; however, if you do not see it listed, you will need to meet with your academic adviser or a professor in the department. I went through this process during my junior/senior year at college. I was very interested in a course that studied terrorism (causes and ways to defeat it), but my university did not offer any. I scheduled a meeting with the chair of the Political Science Department and presented my case. She agreed to do a one-semester independent study with me on this topic.

Of note, you need to go to this meeting absolutely prepared with the exact books/articles you would read throughout the semester(s), what type of assignments you would complete (we agreed on one paper due at the end of the semester), and what you hope to accomplish by completing this independent study. If you fail to have this information prepared when you meet with your academic adviser/professor, do not be surprised if he or she rejects this option. Being prepared will highlight your sincere interest, and it shows that you will be completing actual work throughout the semester.

In addition to finding courses that will assist you in landing your desired job, another option offered by most colleges is studying abroad. Most students who choose this option study abroad for a semester in a country that has courses/internships that align with their desired career field. If you are interested in this possibility, I recommend researching online where the top programs/courses are for your field. You should also discuss this with your academic advisers, mentors, and professors to understand whether this will assist you in the long run. If your desired career field has a global aspect, such as business or marketing, this may be a great step you can take to make yourself more marketable.

Studying abroad is a huge undertaking and your decision should be well thought out. I decided to study abroad in Egypt. This was my first time traveling to another country, and I can honestly say that I had no idea what I was getting myself into. Because I chose Egypt, which is not a typical country most students choose to study abroad in, there was not a well-defined program in place. This was both a very difficult and very rewarding experience. Rewarding in the aspect that this signified my independence and showed me what my personal limits were. It was difficult because I was away from home, family, and friends, and in a place that I was not comfortable in. However, I knew that I was there for a purpose. So I stayed to complete the required credits I needed, and then I went home and started my internship early. Suffice it to say, ensure that the location you choose has a well-defined program to assist you, and that you are as prepared as you can be prior to making this decision and studying abroad. Two websites you may want to look at to begin your research are studiesabroad.com and study-abroad.com, both of which can help you identify a study abroad program that fits your needs.[47,48] There are several online websites to assist with this, and your college may also have a preferred website or even a department dedicated to this on campus, so be sure to speak to your academic adviser about how to begin research on where you can study.

Alongside studying abroad, I recommend that you study a foreign language during college no matter which major/career you select. As noted in a 2011 *US News & World Report* article, "thanks to the proliferation of advanced communications technology, international borders are rapidly dissolving in the professional world. American businesses are now focused on tapping massive emerging markets in China and India, and leaders in those markets have their eyes peeled for young talent who can immediately flourish in a foreign setting."[49] Depending on your major(s), foreign languages may not be a requirement that you need to fulfill for graduation; however, this is a key way you can make yourself more marketable by adding a skill set that sets you apart from the competition. This same *US News & World Report* further suggests that you choose languages that are "in-demand" and that you study abroad to further enhance your language skills in a real-world setting.[50] Throughout my time at undergraduate college I studied three languages: Arabic, Russian, and Spanish. Keep in mind that one of my majors was international studies, which required some foreign language courses. Suffice it to say you do not need to study multiple languages unless that is specifically required for your major or career field.

Even if you do not reach fluency in the languages you study, it will still help set you apart from the competition, as you have already attained some knowledge related to the language(s). I recommend that you take at least two years of a foreign language while in college. This will show that you have the patience and determination to follow through on a language (versus someone who only takes a year and decides that is enough). Languages are difficult to learn; they take constant practice and attention. While this may be more difficult for you to keep your grades up, employers should take note of the level of difficulty and the attention to detail that all languages require, particularly as you move beyond the beginner level courses. Additional languages studied should never diminish your chances at an internship or full-time position; they can only enhance your chances.

The last option that you may want to consider to make yourself more marketable is research. No matter what your major, chances are at least one of your professors will be conducting research during your tenure at college. Offer to assist for free. You could also try to form an independent study out of this so you can claim credit, but be prepared to offer free hours to assist. Not only will you be in a position to learn about official research, you will be working with someone active in your desired career field, both of which are critical to making yourself more marketable, as you will be gaining actual experience. As mentioned earlier, I was able to assist one of my political science professors with research during college and it was a great experience. It also happens to be a line item on my resume to this day. As I explained earlier, research is a critical skill set that spans several career fields. I know that your time is very valuable throughout college, but this is an important option that should not be overlooked. Once you have secured your spot in assisting with the research, you may want to use some of those core curriculum/easy courses in the same time frame that you are conducting research to balance out your hours (this assumes that the easier courses will not require as much out-of-class time).

I would also recommend that you choose your elective courses wisely. While there may be several fun and easy courses, you must constantly be thinking of your end goal: obtaining a job in your desired career field. A 2012 Forbes article suggests that students should consider taking courses in economics, statistics, computer programming, calculus I, communications, and financial planning and management, as they "provide useful knowledge and techniques, but they also signal to potential employers that the student has taken hard subjects."[51] Each of these courses further highlights basic skill sets that are present in several career fields and skill sets that can only improve an employer's impression of you.

MAKING YOURSELF MARKETABLE CHECKLIST

- ✓ You need to set yourself apart from the competition

- ✓ Excel at your internships

- ✓ School papers can be included in resumes and during interviews

- ✓ Take special courses during college

- ✓ Develop an independent study

- ✓ Study abroad

- ✓ Study a foreign language

- ✓ Assist professors with research

BUILDING YOUR RESUME

Beginning your freshman year, and as you progress through college and your internships, you need to build up your resume. This will assist with making yourself marketable and ultimately landing interviews. Your resume is the first and only item a potential employer will see to determine whether to offer you an interview. If you use your network to try to obtain jobs, your network colleague(s) might put in a good word for you, but you can't count on that. Thus, your resume is the only assured item that a potential employer will see.

I have two rules for resumes that must always be adhered to. The first is simple: never lie on a resume. Lying includes stretching the truth. You should only ever tell the truth on a resume. If you do not, you risk ruining your credibility, burning several bridges, and losing the opportunity to work at the company you provided false information to. Despite this very basic rule, from time to time reports are publicized that high-profile individuals have lied on their resumes. It never ends well for these people. Even more so because they are high profile, and now anyone paying attention to the news is aware of what they did. So while this may be more common than not, that does not make it right, and you risk everything when you lie on a resume. The second rule is: keep it concise. For those of you in college, you should be able to keep your resume to one page. For those of you who have already started your career, you need to keep it under two pages. I am in the fifth year of my career and have just expanded to a second page despite my best efforts to keep it to one page. My reason here is quite simple: potential employers will most likely be reading through several resumes and you want to keep yours short and to the point. If you have an incredibly long resume, a potential employer might not read it in its entirety. Following on this point, any line items that you consider the most important information about you should be listed at the top, not the bottom. Additional rules, which should go without stating, are checking for typos and using a professional layout. This means having at least two people read through your resume for typos and intent (oftentimes the way you explain something makes sense to you, but when another person reads through the resume it doesn't come across as you intended). This also means sticking to the basics: automatic font color, no atypical fonts, etc. This does not mean that you have to stick to a basic format. There are several formats and templates available online, and I recommend you find one that is professional but unique. I have included a very basic resume template as well as corresponding detail below. How you organize your resume is up to you, but be sure to list the most recent activity at the top of each category first.

Table 5. Example Resume Template

FIRST NAME LAST NAME	
(111) 111-1111 firstname.lastname@_.com Address	

EDUCATION

School Name	Date Received
Name of Degree Received	
Related Coursework:	
School Name	Date Received
Name of Degree Received	
Related Coursework:	

EXPERIENCE

Company Name	Date Employed
Job Title	
Brief job description with key words	
Company Name	Date Employed
Job Title	
Brief job description with key words	
Research	Date Employed
Job Title/Research Detail	
Brief description with key words	

SKILLS/TRAINING

- Professional certificates
- Excellent communication skills

Here are the basic categories I have on my personal resume that I recommend you include as well: contact information (name, address, e-mail, phone number), education (schools and associated degrees, majors and minors, related coursework, languages studied, any honors you received), and additional education such as certificates, experience, and skills and training. What you include in each section is up to you; however, I highly recommend you include relevant coursework for your career field as it will add details to the degree you are pursuing or have completed. I also recommend you add dates next to each major item. For example, next to my master's degree I have August 2012 to illustrate that I received my advanced degree in August 2012. By adding dates you can add any current degrees or certificates you are currently pursuing but have not yet completed. Rather than an exact date, you can use the phrase "expected August 2013" for example. This will show an employer that you are currently working toward a degree and that you have a known time frame for completing it.

Regarding your contact information, be sure to include an e-mail address that is professional. Several individuals maintain the same e-mail address over the course of several years. This e-mail may include a username that coincides with a nickname. From an employer perspective, everything listed on that resume counts as a point for you or a point against you. So, if you have what someone might consider to be an unprofessional e-mail address, simply create a new e-mail address that includes only your name (and a series of numbers if the e-mail you want is already taken). Similar to this, be sure that you have a professional voicemail on the phone number you include on your resume. I recommend going with the default voicemail. Otherwise use a very basic voicemail that includes your first and last name and says that you will return the call as soon as possible.

The experience category is where you include any relevant professional experience you have acquired. This would include internships and any official research you assisted with. Alternatively, you could create a separate category for research as I have done on my own resume. For each item you include in experience you want to include a brief description of what you accomplished.

The skills and training category highlights any basic skills you currently have such as operating Microsoft Word, excellent communication skills, etc.

The best advice I can give you for a resume, aside from not lying and keeping it concise, is to utilize key words. Understanding which key words are associated with your desired career field is an important factor in getting your resume taken seriously. To figure out which key words are critical in your field, you will need to look at current job openings under the required and preferred requirements as well as talking to advisers, mentors, and colleagues. For example, if you are applying to become a teacher of any sort, you should absolutely utilize key words associated with teaching such as education and training. While this may seem like common sense, be sure to understand if any of your qualifications can be worded differently (without lying or stretching the truth) to better align with your desired career field.

When you are first starting out your resume will be short, and that is absolutely fine. Do not attempt to fluff up your resume with false or irrelevant information. Once you complete your first internship you will have something substantive to add under the experience category and can build from there. I recommend that you keep your resume updated as you go throughout college and your career. You never know when an opportunity will present itself and you do not want to waste any time updating your resume. I review and update my resume twice a year and recommend that you do the same, more often if you have new information to add throughout the year.

BUILDING YOUR RESUME CHECKLIST

✓ Your resume is your first impression, make it count

✓ Never lie on a resume

✓ Keep resume to one page if possible, do not exceed two pages

✓ Utilize key words

GRADUATE SCHOOL

As you are finishing your undergraduate college education, chances are you have thought about graduate school. Particularly in this economy (as I write this chapter it is February 2013), several students have chosen to continue their education in hopes that the job market will be better by the time they graduate with an advanced degree. The problem with this method is that in most cases, these students are footing the bill for their advanced degree in addition to their undergraduate degree. The only time you should consider going to graduate school immediately following your undergraduate education is if you have full scholarships to pay for it. Under no circumstances should you put your undergraduate student loans on hold (also known as deferment) in order to attend graduate school. The Federal Student Aid website defines deferment as "a period during which repayment of the principal and interest of your loan is temporarily delayed." It further stipulates that only with certain federal loans will the government pay the interest on the loan while it is in deferment.[52] The last thing you want to do is add to your student loan debt before you have a full-time job and have had sufficient time to begin paying down your undergraduate student loan debt.

As you are looking at the possibility of graduate school, you should first determine whether an advanced degree is required for your career field. Some simply do not require an advanced degree, particularly for entry-level positions. You can conduct online searches to discover this information. I would also suggest looking at online job websites such as Monster.com.[53] Look specifically at the jobs you want to have and what the requirements are. Pay attention to the required versus preferred information on the job listings. If an advanced degree, such as a master's degree is listed as required, you have your answer. If you do not see advanced degrees under the required information, it may not be necessary to obtain an advanced degree before heading into your career field. I would double-check these results by discussing with your professors, academic advisers, and mentors from your internships as well as looking at several job openings over the course of several months before making a final decision. The decision to attend graduate school should not be an impulse decision, but a well-thought-out conclusion.

Unless your career field dictates that you must have additional education before obtaining a job (e.g., doctor or lawyer) I strongly discourage you from attending graduate school immediately following your undergraduate college. There are a few reasons for this. Most importantly, school is expensive. Graduate school is no exception. If you wait until you have a full-time position, there is a greater chance that you can reduce the cost of graduate school. Several employers offer tuition assistance, either in part or in whole. This should be an important factor that you look into when accepting full-time positions, assuming that attending graduate school is important to you. When I switched companies a few months after accepting my first full-time position, their tuition assistance was a big factor. At the time they covered 100 percent of education with no retention or tuition caps. In essence, they would pay the full cost of any additional education without any gotchas or follow-on requirements from me. Shortly after I joined this company, the tuition assistance changed. They would still pay for my graduate degree, but capped the yearly tuition and required that I stay on for two years after completing my degree or else I would owe them the money back. This is more typical of what you should expect from companies offering tuition assistance. Typically there will be a monetary cap per year along with a retention plan requiring you to stay with the company for a certain period after you finish your education. Suffice it to say, if you can enter into the working world sooner rather than later, start getting paid, and get someone else to pay for your graduate school in part or in whole, you are in great shape.

Another reason you may not want to go to graduate school immediately following your undergraduate education is the barrier to entry in the job market. This completely depends on the current economic environment, so it is important to understand how difficult it is to obtain a job at the time you are graduating. Currently in early 2013, the job market is incredibly difficult and unemployment is high compared to previous years. Having a graduate degree makes you more expensive (typically by correlating to a higher salary), and companies might actually prefer to hire someone without a graduate degree simply to save them money. They may think that an advanced degree is not needed for the job and you are, in fact, overqualified. Or even if an advanced degree is typically required, budget cuts may cause them to reevaluate this requirement for someone with an undergraduate degree and significant potential. I am not trying to dissuade you from graduate school, but rather point out that timing is critical. If you can save yourself thousands of dollars by waiting a year or two, you should consider that option.

At this point, if you still believe that an advanced degree is a good step for you and the timing is right, the next decision you have to make is whether you should attend an in-person school or take advantage of an online program. I briefly mentioned this in an earlier chapter, but I will go into a little more detail here.

Online graduate school is largely dependent on your field. You will need to ask around, talk to colleagues, and find out what is typical within the field. I myself had grand plans of applying to Ivy League schools up until my employer switched the tuition assistance program and capped the yearly amount. Looking at the out-of-pocket amount I would have to pay quickly changed my mind. I started looking at online programs and was able to find an accredited program that fit my needs at the time. If you decide to pursue an online program, research the school to ensure it is accredited and that employers will recognize your degree. Accreditation information can easily be found on the school's website. You can then research the independent accreditations to see which are the most critical for your field. You may also want to take a look at http://ope.ed.gov/accreditation/ which is provided by the US Department of Education and allows you to look up accreditations by school or download all accreditations across all schools.[54]

Once you have decided whether to attend in person or online, you must once again decide what to get your degree in. Some choose to pursue their advanced degrees in a specialized area within their career fields. Others choose to go with a more generic degree such as a master's of business administration (MBA), which spans several career fields. I recommend that you obtain your advanced degree in a different area than your undergraduate degree, as this will make you more marketable to employers and enhance your skill sets in new areas.

GRADUATE SCHOOL CHECKLIST

✓ Do not go to graduate school immediately following undergraduate degree completion

✓ Determine whether your career field requires an advanced degree

✓ Find an employer who offers tuition assistance for advanced degrees

✓ A graduate degree may work against you, depending on the economy

✓ Determine in-person versus online education

✓ Ensure the graduate school you plan to attend is accredited

LANDING A JOB

If you have followed along this far and been able to adhere to the guidelines outlined in previous chapters, landing a job should be relatively easy at this point. As I mentioned earlier, assuming you excel at your internships, you should see a job offer from at least one of the internships. If you decide to look elsewhere for a full-time position, keep in mind that the experience gained from your internships is crucial and will help you land a position by setting you apart from the competition.

The timing of when to begin searching for a full-time position after graduation is absolutely critical. Several of my friends waited until their final semester to get serious about finding a job. I consider this last minute. You are decreasing your odds of getting a full-time position simply because several students wait until the final semester to start looking, thereby increasing the number of applicants applying for available positions. After your first internship you should have a good idea of whether you are headed in a career direction that you will be good at and enjoy. If you find that you did not enjoy your internship, you still have time to find a different section within the career field to try for your second internship. After your second internship you should have a more detailed impression about where exactly you would like to work full-time. It is at this point that you should begin to make a list of possible companies/organizations that you would be interested in working at full-time. For most people, the second internship should be completed in the summer between junior and senior year. Therefore, if you start looking for full-time positions in the August before you graduate, you have nearly a full year to land a job. It is never too early to start looking for a job. Several companies will also offer you the job during your senior year that is contingent upon your graduation (meaning that if you fail to graduate they will rescind their job offer). I accepted my job offer the fall before I graduated. I later decided to graduate early and requested an earlier start date with the company, which they agreed to.

I recommend that you take that list of companies and add to it over the course of one month. By the time September comes around you should have a condensed list of ten to twenty companies. Depending on the economic environment at the time you are preparing to graduate, you may want to increase the number of companies you apply to. While this may sound like a significant undertaking, remember that this will assist you in landing a job, and hopefully multiple job offers. Never assume that you can apply to one company and land a job. You should always have backup plans in place. You should also discuss with your mentors and advisers which companies you are thinking of applying to. Chances are they will have some insight to offer you on at least a few of the companies.

With your condensed list of companies in hand, you need to look at each of their websites online and learn more about the company. This process is similar to when you researched colleges to attend: you need to look at locations, benefits, and the process to apply. Generally speaking, you want to find an employer who offers good health insurance and a retirement plan such as a 401k. If you plan to attend graduate school or any other additional school at some point, you will want to ensure that they offer tuition assistance as well. All of the previously mentioned items are important, but in your first job you may not have multiple options to choose from. So do not be too picky. Chances are you will not stay with your first company until retirement so once you have built up experience, you can always look to transfer companies and be a little more selective based on the health care, retirement, and tuition packages they offer. If you do have multiple job offers and are having a hard time choosing between the two, look closely at these additional packages to help you decide.

In order to land a job, you need a resume. As I mentioned above, the best advice I can give you on your resume is to keep it at one page if possible, and certainly not over two pages. I've found (and been told by employers) that they will lose interest quickly. Short and to the point is the way to go. My current resume has finally spilled over one page, just by a few lines. And this is after two internships, two full-time positions with two companies, research I conducted in college, both my undergraduate degree and my graduate degree. I have tried very hard to keep it to one page. If you are having trouble fitting everything into one page, play with the margins and font, but remember to keep it legible and within the print range, particularly since you will likely be applying online (you don't want an employer to receive your resume electronically and print it out only to discover part of it got cut off). If you have to squint to read the resume you are going to frustrate possible employers.

Another important aspect with resumes that took me years to realize is that key words are everything when it comes to resumes. To determine which key words are critical to your career field you will need to conduct online research, talk to your academic advisers, and mentors from your internships. As most anyone will tell you, under no circumstances do you ever lie on your resume. But you should be sure to utilize the correct terminology in describing your experience that matches up with your career field.

Even if you interned with the company you want to work for, you may have to interview for the position, particularly if it is in a different department than you interned with. You must prepare for any interview as if your life depended on it. Your internships got your foot in the door, but the interview will make or break the pending job offer. You absolutely must wear a suit on the day of the interview and come prepared with at least two copies of your resume. Prior to the actual interview, you should also be practicing interview questions. You can expect the basic questions such as "tell me about yourself" and "why do you think you would be a good fit for this position?" But you need to go further in depth and be prepared for the unexpected questions. Based on the position you are applying for you should also do additional research on topics they might question you about. For example, if you are applying for a research position at a law firm that specializes in criminal defense, it would behoove you to be up to speed on recent cases in the news on this topic and how you would have researched this case. You need to impress the person you are interviewing with. Show them that this is not just a job to you; this is your passion. When I was in the process of interviewing for my first internship (the nonprofit organization in Washington, DC) I was forewarned that there would be questions about current events and policy. That was not a lot to go on, so my friends helped me cover stacks of policy papers available online and current events. We literally spent hours over the course of two weeks preparing. And sure enough when the questions came in the interview I was prepared and was offered the internship.

At my current company, I recently interviewed for a different position internal to the company. I knew that several of my colleagues were applying for this same position, at least one of whom had more years of experience than I. Therefore, I prepared as if my life depended on it. Not only did I come to the interview with my updated resume, I had two letters of recommendation (specific for this interview) from a supervisor at my current position and a team at my current position that I worked with extensively. I also prepared a brief paper describing exactly how I would execute my duties if I were selected for this position. Between these documents and my preparation for the interview questions I was offered the position. I strongly believe that my significant preparation played a huge role in this. So while this may seem excessive, it worked. If it helps you land that job then it is absolutely worth all the time and effort that went into preparation.

Since this is likely your first job, letters of recommendation may be difficult to obtain. I would recommend reaching out to your internships to see if anyone there would be willing to write a letter of recommendation. If that is not an option, check with some of your favorite professors from classes that you have excelled in. Be sure to give these individuals ample time to write the recommendation for you, at least three weeks' advance notice.

Depending on the company you are interviewing with, you may not have enough information to be able to prepare a brief paper that details how you would execute your duties. If this is the case, you should still strive to prepare a short paper that illustrates how you would assist in their core business areas. For example, if you are interviewing for an information technology position, you should conduct research on new technologies or strategies that could benefit the company you are interviewing for. Whether the company is currently using this information or not, you are still showing that you have prepared for this interview and have a desire to see the company succeed. Be careful that you are not promoting any competitor products or services in this short paper.

In addition to the documents that you will bring to the interview (be sure to bring more than one copy of each document in case additional individuals sit in on the interview), you need to prepare for the questions you will be asked. A 2013 Forbes article lists fifty common interview questions that you can prepare for and further suggests that "job seekers need to anticipate less conventional interview questions, and that they should think of oddball queries as an opportunity to demonstrate their thought process, to communicate their values and character, and to show the prospective employer how they perform under pressure."[55] A separate 2013 Forbes article relieves some of the stress associated with unanticipated questions by stating that "the bottom line is that the employer doesn't expect you to know how many cows are in Canada (asked by Google), or how many windows are in New York (asked by Bain & Co.)—but they will be pleased to know that you've done your homework and you can think fast."[56]

I would also be prepared with a few questions of your own to ask during the interview. It is not uncommon for the person(s) interviewing you to ask if you have any questions. Have two or three well-thought-out questions to highlight that you really have thought about this position and what it would mean to you. Examples of these questions could include: What training opportunities would be available to me in this position to help advance my career within the company? Does the company currently have a mentoring program to assist new hires in excelling throughout their first year with the company?

Since this will be your first full-time position in the career field of your choice, it is important to once again remember that you are just starting out. You need to be realistic. Don't expect to immediately be offered your dream salary. I myself was horrified when I received my offer in the mail at half the salary I was hoping for. This was devastating to me because I had interned with this company and excelled in every way possible. One of my supervisors even referred to me as a rock star based on my performance.

Suffice it to say, no matter how great you are, chances are you will get a low salary offer. And because this is your first position, you don't have a lot of negotiating room. Despite your two internships, the companies will offer you a salary on the lower end, claiming lack of experience. While the internships set you apart from the competition, they do not guarantee you a hefty salary.

This is a delicate balance. I went back and was able to negotiate a small amount higher, but this still left me significantly short of my dream salary.

My advice to you is to note that while you are being offered a lower salary, you are still better off than the competition that wasn't offered a salary at all. I recommend that you try to negotiate, very diplomatically, to raise their offer slightly. Every little bit counts. Also be sure to have a legitimate reason for asking for a little bit more. Simply stating that you think you are worth more will get you nowhere and might, in fact, cost you the job offer. If you have done the math and legitimately don't believe you can cover your cost of living, that is a much more compelling reason to communicate to the employer. More importantly, within six months at this full-time position, you have already gained that real-world experience and other companies will take notice. A few months into my first full-time position, another company took notice, and after a lengthy decision process on my end, I decided to switch companies. This was the best career decision I have made. While there are certainly no guarantees when it comes to switching companies, if you do your research about both companies and the opportunities you will have with both, you should be able to arrive at an answer on whether to switch companies.

And as you switch companies you can expect your salary to jump upward now that you have some experience. When I switched companies after only six months, my salary jumped over 38 percent. A friend of mine who is a few years younger and in a different industry altogether waited almost a year before switching companies and her salary jumped over 50 percent.

Suffice it to say, don't expect your dream salary on your first job offer. This will come within the first few years provided you continue to excel at your job and are willing to put in the hours to outshine the competition.

LANDING A JOB CHECKLIST

✓ Start applying for jobs the year before you graduate

✓ Apply to at least ten jobs

✓ Prepare for interviews as if your life depended on it

✓ Don't expect a dream salary at your first job

CONCLUSION

Pursuing a college degree is an exciting and rewarding undertaking. Be realistic with the colleges you choose to apply to. Take the time necessary to research multiple schools until you find ten options that match your needs. Ensure that they are financially feasible based on the salary you will receive as an entry-level employee in your desired career field. Do not ever attend an expensive school on the assumption that you will obtain a job to cover the cost of your student loans. Make time to apply for several scholarships to reduce the overall cost of your college education. Your goal should be to go to college for free. If you are unable to acquire enough scholarships, you will need to apply for student loans, but remember that these are legal contracts and you will be obligated to repay these loans according to the agreed upon schedule and terms.

Once you get to college, remember that you are on a mission, and freshman year is your time to get ahead. Select an academic adviser who is active in his or her field as early as possible. Be sure to fight for any college credit from applicable high school (or other) courses, and utilize your college course handbook to find and employ shortcuts among your required courses.

Between your sophomore and senior years you must strive to obtain and excel at two internships. This will help you begin your professional network, make yourself more marketable, and obtain job offers. Remember that internships are your first impression in the professional realm so make them count; outshine the competition and be willing to put in the long hours. If you are struggling to land your first internship, offer to assist professors with research to gain practical experience. Once you land your first internship, your second internship should be much easier to acquire.

As you progress throughout college, take advantage of term papers and choose paper topics that correlate to relevant topics in your desired career field. These can then be mentioned in your resume and during interviews. Consider studying a foreign language and studying abroad to further separate you from the competition and make yourself more marketable to employers.

Resumes are your first impression to a potential employer so keep it professional and concise. One page is preferable, but two will suffice. Never lie on your resume. Employ key words to make your resume stand out.

Think carefully about attending graduate school. Timing is critical; it is best if you can find a job immediately following undergraduate school where the employer offers tuition assistance for graduate school. Depending on the economy, a graduate degree may work against you landing a job. Weigh all the options before you make a decision one way or another regarding graduate school.

As with internships, apply early and often for post-graduation full-time positions. Prepare for your interviews as if your life depended on it. You need to be memorable and show that you would be a great employee. Be realistic with your expectations about your salary at your first job.

College is what you make it. The guidelines outlined in this book should help you avoid the common pitfalls most students experience. Never let rejection keep you from your dream career. Planning ahead, working hard, and being determined are truly the keys to college success.

BIBLIOGRAPHY

"America's Navy—A Global Force for Good: Navy.com."
Navy.com. Accessed February 10, 2013. http://
www.navy.com/.

"Amortization Schedule Calculator—Bankrate.com."
Bankrate.com. Accessed February 10, 2013. http://
www.bankrate.com/calculators/college-planning/
loan-calculator.aspx.

"AP Central—Advanced Placement Scores, Courses
& Exam Center | AP Central—APC Members
Home." *CollegeBoard*. Accessed February 10, 2013.
http://apcentral.collegeboard.com
/apc/Controller.jpf.

"AP Central—Course Descriptions." *CollegeBoard*.
Accessed February 10, 2013. http://apcentral.
collegeboard.com/apc/public/courses/descriptions/
index.html.

"AP Central—Exam Fees and Reductions: 2013." *CollegeBoard*. Accessed February 10, 2013. http://apcentral.collegeboard.com/apc/public/exam/calendar/190165.html.

"Apartments.com." *Apartments.com*. Accessed February 10, 2013. http://www.apartments.com.

Burnsed, Brian. "4 Tips to Learn a Foreign Language in College: Study Abroad If You're Serious About Learning A Language." *US News & World Report* (February 9, 2011). http://www.usnews.com/education/best-colleges/articles/2011/02/09/4-tips-to-learn-a-foreign-language-in-college.

"CollegeView.com—College Finder and Recruiting Service." *CollegeView*. Accessed February 10, 2013. http://www.collegeview.com/index.jsp.

Conerly, Bill. "The Six Classes That Will Make Any College Grad Employable." *Forbes* (August 21, 2012). http://www.forbes.com/sites/billconerly/2012/08/21/how-to-make-a-college-graduate-employable/.

"Cost of Living Comparison Calculator." *Bankrate*. Accessed February 10, 2013. http://www.bankrate.com/calculators/savings/moving-cost-of-living-calculator.aspx.

Couch, Christina. "5 Colleges You Can Go to for Free."
    Yahoo! Finance (January 11, 2013).
    http://finance.yahoo.com/news/5-colleges-you-can-
    go-to-for-free-185652 815.html.

"Craigslist." *Craigslist*. Accessed February 10, 2013.
    http://www.craigslist.org/about/sites/.

"Decrease in Overall Debt Balance Continues Despite Rise
    in Non-Real Estate Debt." *Federal Reserve Bank
    of New York* (November 27, 2012). http://www.
    newyorkfed.org/newsevents/news/research/2012/
    an121127.html.

"Deferment and Forbearance | Federal Student
    Aid." *Federal Student Aid: An Office of the US
    Department of Education*. Accessed February 18,
    2013. http://studentaid.ed.gov/repay-loans/
    deferment-forbearance.

"FAFSA—Free Application for Federal Student Aid."
    FAFSA on the Web. Accessed February 10, 2013.
    http://www.fafsa.ed.gov/.

"Fastweb: Scholarships, Financial Aid, Student Loans and
    Colleges." *Fastweb*. Accessed February 10, 2013.
    http://www.fastweb.com/.

"FinAid | Calculators | Loan Calculator." *FinAid*. Accessed
    February 10, 2013. http://www.finaid.org/
    calculators/loanpayments.phtml.

"FinAid! Financial Aid, College Scholarships and Student Loans." *FinAid*. Accessed February 10, 2013. http://www.finaid.org/.

"Find Internships | Intern Jobs | Paid Internships." *InternMatch*. Accessed February 10, 2013. http://www.internmatch.com/.

"Find Internships at Top Companies—MonsterCollege™." *MonsterCollege*. Accessed February 10, 2013. http://college.monster.com/education.

"Find Jobs. Build a Better Career. Find Your Calling. | Monster.com." *Monster*. Accessed February 10, 2013. http://www.monster.com/.

"Forgiveness, Cancellation, and Discharge | Federal Student Aid." *Federal Student Aid: An Office of the US Department of Education*. Accessed February 18, 2013. http://studentaid.ed.gov/repay-loans/forgiveness-cancellation#teacher-loan.

"Go Army Homepage." *GoArmy.com*. Accessed February 10, 2013. http://www.goarmy.com/cl3.html.

"Grants and Scholarships | Federal Student Aid." *Federal Student Aid: An Office of the US Department of Education*. Accessed February 10, 2013. http://studentaid.ed.gov/types/grants-scholarships.

"Half.com—Textbooks, Books, CDs, Movies, More." *Half. com*. Accessed February 10, 2013. http://www.half. ebay.com/.

"Internal Revenue Service." *IRS*. Accessed February 10, 2013. http://www.irs.gov/.

"International Education—The International Baccalaureate Offers High Quality Programmes of Education to a Worldwide Community of Schools." *Ibo.org*. Accessed February 10, 2013. http://www.ibo.org/.

"International Studies Abroad." *International Studies Abroad*. Accessed February 10, 2013. http:// studiesabroad.com/.

"LendingTree Ranks the 50 United States According to Average Monthly Mortgage Payment." *PR Newswire* (November 27, 2012). http://www. prnewswire.com/news-releases/lendingtree-ranks-the-50-united-states-according-to-average-monthly-mortgage-payment-180992531. html and http://marketing.lendingtree.com/pr/ national_average_payment.pdf.

"Loans | Federal Student Aid." *Federal Student Aid: An Office of the US Department of Education.* Accessed February 10, 2013. http://studentaid.ed.gov/types/ loans.

Loretto, Penny. "Penny's Top Internship Sites for 2013." *About.com Internships*. Accessed February 10, 2013. http://internships.about.com/od/internsites/tp/internsites.htm.

Lorin, Janet. "Yale Suing Former Students Shows Crisis in Loans to Poor." *Bloomberg* (February 5, 2013). http://www.bloomberg.com/news/2013-02-05/yale-suing-former-students-shows-crisis-in-loans-to-poor.html.

Miller, Joshua Rhett. "$10G Degree Deal: Governors Push State Schools to Offer Bachelor's Bargain." *FoxNews.com* (February 6, 2013). http://www.foxnews.com/us/2013/02/06/more-governors-university-systems-pushing-10g-bachelor-degree/.

"National University Rankings | Top National Universities | US News Best Colleges." *US News & World Report*. Accessed February 10, 2013. http://colleges.usnews.rankingsandreviews.com/best-colleges/rankings/national-universities.

"ROTC Programs—Today's Military." *Today's Military*. Accessed February 10, 2013. http://www.todaysmilitary.com/main/before-serving-in-the-military/rotc-programs.

"Scholarships.com: Free College Scholarship Search | College Recruiting | Financial Aid Information."

Scholarships.com. Accessed February 10, 2013. http://www.scholarships.com/.

Schwartz, Nelson D. "Employers Increasingly Rely on Internal Referrals in Hiring: In Hiring, a Friend in Need Is a Prospect, Indeed." *The New York Times*, sec. Business Day (January 27, 2013). http://www.nytimes.com/2013/01/28/business/ employers-increasingly-rely-on-internal-referrals -in-hiring.html.

Smith, Jacquelyn. "How to Ace the 50 Most Common Interview Questions." *Forbes* (January 11, 2013). http://www.forbes.com/sites/ jacquelynsmith/2013/01/11/how-to-ace-the -50-most-common-interview-questions/.

Smith, Jacquelyn. "The Most Oddball Interview Questions of the Year." *Forbes* (January 11, 2013). http:// www.forbes.com/sites/jacquelynsmith/2013/01/11/ the-most-oddball-interview-questions-of-the-year/.

"StudentsReview: Salaries by Major." *StudentsReview*. Accessed February 10, 2013. http://www. studentsreview.com/salary_by_major.php3.

"Study Abroad.com." *StudyAbroad.com*. Accessed February 10, 2013. http://www.studyabroad.com/default. aspx.

"Tuition and Fee and Room and Board Charges over Time in 2012 Dollars, 1972–73 Through 2012–13, Selected Years." *CollegeBoard*. Accessed February 10, 2013. http://trends.collegeboard.org/college-pricing/figures-tables/tuition-and-fee-and-room-and-board-charges-over-time-1972-73-through-2012-13-selected-years.

"US Department of Education Database of Accredited Postsecondary Institutions and Programs." *US Department of Education*. Accessed February 10, 2013. http://ope.ed.gov/accreditation/.

"United States Air Force—Airforce.com." *US Air Force*. Accessed February 10, 2013. http://www.airforce.com/.

"United States Coast Guard." *United States Coast Guard*. Accessed February 10, 2013. http://www.gocoastguard.com/.

"United States Marine Corps." *Marines.com*. Accessed February 10, 2013. http://www.marines.com/home.

"US News & World Report | News & Rankings | Best Colleges, Best Hospitals, and More." *US News & World Report*. Accessed February 10, 2013. http://www.usnews.com/.

Wecker, Menachem. "10 Colleges With the Highest Application Fees." *US News & World Report* (September 25, 2012). http://www.usnews.com/ education/best-colleges/the-short-list-college/ articles/2012/09/25/10-colleges-with-the-highest-application-fees.

1. Menachem Wecker, "10 Colleges With the Highest Application Fees," *US News & World Report* (September 25, 2012), http://www.usnews.com/education/best-colleges/the-short-list-college/articles/2012/09/25/10-colleges-with-the-highest-application-fees.

2. Wecker, "10 Colleges."

3. "CollegeView.com—College Finder and Recruiting Service," *CollegeView*, accessed February 10, 2013, http://www.collegeview.com/index.jsp.

4. "US News & World Report | News & Rankings | Best Colleges, Best Hospitals, and More," *US News & World Report*, accessed February 10, 2013, http://www.usnews.com/.

5. "Tuition and Fee and Room and Board Charges over Time in 2012 Dollars, 1972–73 Through 2012–13, Selected Years," *CollegeBoard*, accessed February 10, 2013, http://trends.collegeboard.org/college-pricing/figures-tables/tuition-and-fee-and-room-and-board-charges-over-time-1972-73-through-2012-13-selected-years.

6. Janet Lorin, "Yale Suing." Former Students Shows Crisis in Loans to Poor," *Bloomberg*, February 5, 2013, http://www.bloomberg.com/news/2013-02-05/yale-suing-former-students-shows-crisis-in-loans-to-poor.html.

7. Lorin, "Yale Suing."

8. "National University Rankings | Top National Universities | US News Best Colleges," *US News & World Report*, accessed February 10, 2013, http://colleges.usnews.rankingsandreviews.com/best-colleges/rankings/national-universities.

9. "Find Jobs. Build a Better Career. Find Your Calling. | Monster.com," *Monster*, accessed February 10, 2013, http://www.monster.com/.

10. "LendingTree Ranks the 50 United States According to Average Monthly Mortgage Payment," *PR Newswire* (November 27, 2012), http://www.prnewswire.com/news-releases/lendingtree-ranks-the-50-united-states-according-to-average-monthly-mortgage-payment-180992531.html and http://marketing.lendingtree.com/pr/national_average_payment.pdf.

11. "StudentsReview: Salaries by Major," *StudentsReview*, accessed February 10, 2013, http://www.studentsreview.com/salary_by_major.php3.

12. "Apartments.com," *Apartments.com*, accessed February 10, 2013, http://www.apartments.com.

13. "Craigslist," *Craigslist*, accessed February 10, 2013, http://www.craigslist.org/about/sites/.

14. "Cost of Living Comparison Calculator," *Bankrate*, accessed February 10, 2013, http://www.bankrate.com/calculators/savings/moving-cost-of-living-calculator.aspx.

15. "Internal Revenue Service," *IRS*, accessed February 10, 2013, http://www.irs.gov/.

16. "Internal Revenue Service," *IRS*, accessed February 10, 2013, http://www.irs.gov/.

17. "Amortization Schedule Calculator—Bankrate.com," *Bankrate.com*, accessed February 10, 2013, http://www.bankrate.com/calculators/college-planning/loan-calculator.aspx.

18. "FinAid | Calculators | Loan Calculator," *FinAid*, accessed February 10, 2013, http://www.finaid.org/calculators/loanpayments.phtml.

19. "Half.com—Textbooks, Books, CDs, Movies, More," *Half.com*, accessed February 10, 2013, http://www.half.ebay.com/.

20. "Scholarships.com: Free College Scholarship Search | College Recruiting | Financial Aid Information," *Scholarships.com*, accessed February 10, 2013, http://www.scholarships.com/.

21. "Fastweb : Scholarships, Financial Aid, Student Loans and Colleges," *Fastweb*, accessed February 10, 2013, http://www.fastweb.com/.

22. "FinAid! Financial Aid, College Scholarships and Student Loans," *FinAid*, accessed February 10, 2013, http://www.finaid.org/.

23. "ROTC Programs—Today's Military," *Today's Military*, accessed February 10, 2013, http://www.todaysmilitary.com/main/before-serving-in-the-military/rotc-programs.

24. "United States Marine Corps," *Marines.com*, accessed February 10, 2013, http://www.marines.com/home.

25. "United States Air Force—Airforce.com," *US Air Force*, accessed February 10, 2013, http:// www.airforce.com/.

26. "Go Army Homepage," *GoArmy.com*, accessed February 10, 2013, http://www.goarmy.com/cl3.html.

27. "America's Navy—A Global Force for Good: Navy.com," *Navy.com*, accessed February 10, 2013, http://www.navy.com/navy/?campaign=search_Reprise/Google/Navy+Brand/ percent252Bnavy&sid=navy.

28. "United States Coast Guard," *United States Coast Guard*, accessed February 10, 2013, http://www.gocoastguard.com/.

29. Christina Couch, "5 Colleges You Can Go to for Free," *Yahoo! Finance* (January 11, 2013), http://finance.yahoo.com/news/5-colleges-you-can-go-to-for-free-185652815.html.

30. Joshua Rhett Miller, "$10G Degree Deal: Governors Push State Schools to Offer Bachelor's Bargain," *FoxNews.com* (February 6, 2013), http://www.foxnews.com/us/2013/02/06/more-governors-university-systems-pushing-10g-bachelor-degree/.

31. "Decrease in Overall Debt Balance Continues Despite Rise in Non-Real Estate Debt," *Federal Reserve Bank of New York* (November 27, 2012), http://www.newyorkfed.org/newsevents/news/research/2012/an121127.html.

32. "Loans | Federal Student Aid," *Federal Student Aid: An Office of the US Department of Education*, accessed February 10, 2013, http://studentaid.ed.gov/types/loans.

33. "FAFSA—Free Application for Federal Student Aid," *FAFSA on the Web*, accessed February 10, 2013, http://www.fafsa.ed.gov/.

34. "Loans | Federal Student Aid," *Federal Student Aid: An Office of the US Department of Education*, accessed February 10, 2013, http://studentaid.ed.gov/types/loans.

35. "Forgiveness, Cancellation, and Discharge | Federal Student Aid," *Federal Student Aid: An Office of the US Department of Education*, accessed February 18, 2013, http://studentaid.ed.gov/repay-loans/forgiveness-cancellation#teacher-loan.

36. "Grants and Scholarships | Federal Student Aid," *Federal Student Aid: An Office of the US Department of Education*, accessed February 10, 2013, http://studentaid.ed.gov/types/grants-scholarships.

37. "Forgiveness, Cancellation, and Discharge | Federal Student Aid," *Federal Student Aid: An Office of the US Department of Education*, accessed February 18, 2013, http://studentaid. ed.gov/repay-loans/forgiveness-cancellation#teacher-loan.

38. "AP Central—Advanced Placement Scores, Courses & Exam Center | AP Central—APC Members Home," *CollegeBoard*, accessed February 10, 2013, http://apcentral. collegeboard.com/apc/Controller.jpf.

39. "AP Central—Course Descriptions," *CollegeBoard*, accessed February 10, 2013, http://apcentral.collegeboard. com/apc/public/courses/descriptions/index.html.

40. "AP Central—Exam Fees and Reductions: 2013," *CollegeBoard*, accessed February 10, 2013, http://apcentral. collegeboard.com/apc/public/exam/calendar/190165.html.

41. "International Education—The International Baccalaureate Offers High Quality Programmes of Education to a Worldwide Community of Schools," *Ibo. org*, accessed February 10, 2013, http://www.ibo.org/.

42. Nelson D. Schwartz, "Employers Increasingly Rely on Internal Referrals in Hiring: In Hiring, a Friend in Need Is a Prospect, Indeed," *The New York Times*, sec. Business Day (January 27, 2013), http://www.nytimes. com/2013/01/28/business/employers-increasingly-rely-on-internal-referrals-in-hiring.html.

43. Schwartz, "Employers Increasingly Rely."

44. "Find Internships | Intern Jobs | Paid Internships," *InternMatch*, accessed February 10, 2013, http://www. internmatch.com/.

45. "Find Internships at Top Companies— MonsterCollege™," *MonsterCollege*, accessed February 10, 2013, http://college.monster.com/education.

46. Penny Loretto, "Penny's Top Internship Sites for 2013," *About.com Internships*, accessed February 10, 2013, http://internships.about.com/od/internsites/tp/internsites.htm.

47. "International Studies Abroad," *International Studies Abroad*, accessed February 10, 2013, http://studiesabroad.com/.

48. "Study Abroad," *StudyAbroad.com*, accessed February 10, 2013, http://www.studyabroad.com/default.aspx.

49. Brian Burnsed, "4 Tips to Learn a Foreign Language in College: Study Abroad If You're Serious About Learning A Language," *US News & World Report* (February 9, 2011), http://www.usnews.com/education/best-colleges/articles/2011/02/09/4-tips-to-learn-a-foreign-language-in-college.

50. Burnsed, "4 Tips."

51. Bill Conerly, "The Six Classes That Will Make Any College Grad Employable," *Forbes* (August 21, 2012), http://www.forbes.com/sites/billconerly/2012/08/21/how-to-make-a-college-graduate-employable/.

52. "Deferment and Forbearance | Federal Student Aid," *Federal Student Aid: An Office of the US Department of Education*, accessed February 18, 2013, http://studentaid.ed.gov/repay-loans/deferment-forbearance.

53. "Find Jobs. Build a Better Career. Find Your Calling. | Monster.com," *Monster*, accessed February 10, 2013, http://www.monster.com/.

54. "US Department of Education Database of Accredited Postsecondary Institutions and Programs," *US Department of Education*, accessed February 10, 2013, http://ope.ed.gov/accreditation/.

55. Jacquelyn Smith, "How to Ace the 50 Most Common Interview Questions," *Forbes* (January 11, 2013), http://www.forbes.com/sites/jacquelynsmith /2013/01/11/how-to-ace-the-50-most-common-interview-questions/.

56. Jacquelyn Smith, "The Most Oddball Interview Questions of the Year," *Forbes* (January 11, 2013), http://www.forbes.com/sites/jacquelynsmith/2013/01/11/the-most-oddball-interview-questions-of-the-year/.

ABOUT THE AUTHOR

Megan Ann Smith is an Information Technology Project Manager for a Fortune 500 company based in the Washington, DC area. She has a Master's Degree in Intelligence Studies from American Military University and a Bachelor's Degree in Political Science and International Studies from Trinity University. She was able to attend college, graduate a semester early, pay off her student loans in less than two and a half years, and complete her Master's Degree for free, all of which resulted in her being able to achieve her goal of a six-figure salary by the age of twenty-three. *Before Reality Hits: A Straightforward Guide to College Success* shares the secrets of her success.

Made in the USA
Charleston, SC
01 August 2013